# DOVER STAMPING CO.

# DOVER STAMPING CO.

# 1869

---

*Tinware, Tin Toys, Tinned Iron Wares,*
*Tinners' Material, Enameled Stove Hollow Ware,*
*Tinners' Tools and Machines*

Illustrated Catalog and Historical Introduction

AMERICAN HISTORICAL CATALOG COLLECTION

## THE PYNE PRESS
Princeton

*Note to the Reader.* Reproduction of copy and line drawings are as faithful to the original as is technically possible. Broken type and lines which are uneven or broken can be spotted; these are original! You will also find that this edition of the 1869 Dover catalog contains a number of blank and oddly-numbered pages. These, too, are original. You will understand that manufacturers of such products as tinware, wooden-ware, glassware and weathervanes were not dedicated to the fine art of printing or involved in the business of publishing. All American Historical Catalog Collection editions are photographed in facsimile from the best available copy, are printed on an especially receptive offset paper, and are strongly bound.

# DOVER STAMPING COMPANY,

MANUFACTURERS AND DEALERS IN

## TINNERS'

## Hard Ware & Furnishing Goods

## Nos. 88 & 90 NORTH STREET,

BOSTON, MASS.

1869.

PRESS OF HOLLIS & GUNN, 25 HAWLEY STREET, BOSTON.

# TO THE TRADE.

HAVING been long engaged in the manufacture of Stamped Tin Goods, and Tinners' Hardware in general, and believing our efforts have been acceptable to our customers, we feel called upon by frequent enquiries for lists of our manufactures, to issue this, our third Illustrated Catalogue, and we do so with a full determination to sustain for our goods the high character they have borne in times past.

We have endeavored to meet a growing demand for a better quality of FRENCH TINNED GOODS than has hitherto been manufactured in this country, to which end we have made large investments of money, and procured from abroad competent workmen, which we find to have been warranted by the results.

Our French Tinned Iron Goods, in quality and finish, are unequaled, and no pains will be spared to keep them so, while in *variety* it will be our purpose to anticipate the market in the production of new and useful articles.

We trust our experience and devotion to business will be sufficient warrant for the continued confidence of our customers and the trade generally.

Yours,

E. D. GOODRICH.
HORACE WHITNEY.

DOVER STAMPING CO.

*Boston, January,* 1869.

# DOVER STAMPING COMPANY.

## CATALOGUE.

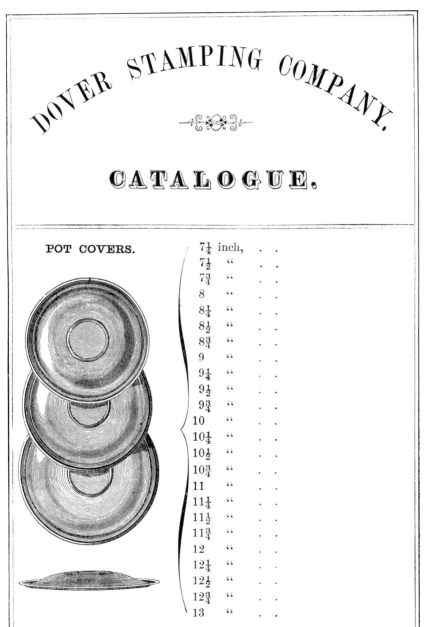

**POT COVERS.**

| | |
|---|---|
| 7¼ inch, | . . |
| 7½ " | . . |
| 7¾ " | . . |
| 8 " | . . |
| 8¼ " | . . |
| 8½ " | . . |
| 8¾ " | . . |
| 9 " | . . |
| 9¼ " | . . |
| 9½ " | . . |
| 9¾ " | . . |
| 10 " | . . |
| 10¼ " | . . |
| 10½ " | . . |
| 10¾ " | . . |
| 11 " | . . |
| 11¼ " | . . |
| 11½ " | . . |
| 11¾ " | . . |
| 12 " | . . |
| 12¼ " | . . |
| 12½ " | . . |
| 12¾ " | . . |
| 13 " | . . |

Measured from base of the bead to correspond with the *inside* measure of the article to be covered. The flanges *outside* the bead cover the edge of the Pot or Kettle, and complete a perfect fit. Our covers are raised much higher than any other, giving them more than double strength, and a symmetrical finish to the article covered.

## PAIL or BUCKET COVERS.

OUTSIDE MEASURE.

| | | |
|---|---|---|
| 1 Pint, | $4\frac{1}{8}$ inch, | . |
| 1 Quart, | 5 " | . |
| 2 " | $6\frac{1}{8}$ " | . |
| 2 " | $6\frac{1}{4}$ " | . |
| 2 ×3 " | $6\frac{3}{8}$ " | . |
| 3 " | $6\frac{1}{2}$ " | . |
| 4 " | 7 " | . |
| 5 " | $7\frac{3}{4}$ " | . |
| 6 " | $8\frac{1}{2}$ " | . |
| 8 " | 9 " | . |
| 10 " | $9\frac{5}{8}$ " | . |
| 12 " | $10\frac{1}{2}$ " | . |

## BUCKET COVERS.

IX TIN.

| | | | | | |
|---|---|---|---|---|---|
| 8 inch, | . | . | . | . | . |
| $8\frac{1}{2}$ " | . | . | . | . | . |
| $8\frac{3}{4}$ " | . | . | . | . | . |
| 9 " | . | . | . | . | . |
| $9\frac{3}{8}$ " | . | . | . | . | . |
| $9\frac{1}{2}$ " | . | . | . | . | . |
| $9\frac{3}{4}$ " | . | . | . | . | . |
| 10 " | . | . | . | . | . |
| $10\frac{3}{8}$ " | . | . | . | . | . |
| $10\frac{1}{2}$ " | . | . | . | . | . |
| $10\frac{7}{8}$ " | . | . | . | . | . |
| 11 " | . | . | . | . | . |
| $11\frac{1}{8}$ " | . | . | . | . | . |
| $11\frac{1}{4}$ " | . | . | . | . | . |
| $11\frac{3}{8}$ " | . | . | . | . | . |
| $11\frac{1}{2}$ " | . | . | . | . | . |
| $11\frac{3}{4}$ " | . | . | . | . | . |
| 12 " | . | . | . | . | . |
| $12\frac{1}{2}$ " | . | . | . | . | . |
| 13 " | . | . | . | . | . |

Measure from extreme edges. To be used with a rim.
An excellent cover for first-class Ware.

## STEAMER BOTTOMS.

OUTSIDE MEASURE.

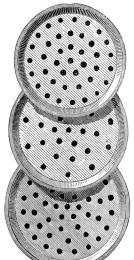

$9\frac{1}{2}$ inches, . . . . .

$\quad 9\frac{3}{4}$ " . . . .

$\quad 10\frac{1}{2}$ " . . . .

$\quad 11$ " . . . .

$\quad 11\frac{1}{4}$ " . . . .

$\quad 11\frac{1}{2}$ " . . . .

The extreme outside measure of Ware should indicate size wanted.

## TEA-KETTLE BREASTS & COVERS.

OUTSIDE MEASURE.

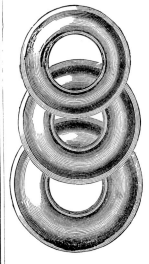

$6$ inch, . . .

$\quad 6\frac{1}{2}$ " . . .

$\quad 7$ " . . .

$\quad 7\frac{1}{2}$ " . . .

$\quad 8$ " . . .

$\quad 8\frac{1}{2}$ " . . .

$\quad 9$ " . . .

$\quad 9\frac{1}{2}$ " . . .

$\quad 10$ " . . .

$\quad 10\frac{1}{2}$ " . . .

$\quad 11$ " . . .

$\quad 11\frac{1}{2}$ " . . .

$\quad 12$ " . . .

## TOILET JAR FIXTURES.

### FLUTED COVERS.

Diam.

Fluted Covers, 10½ in.
Bottom or F't, 7½ top.
Cesspools,        3⅝ in.
SETS, . . . . . .

## SPUN TIN PIPE COLLARS.

### DIAMETER OF HOLE.

4 inch, Spun, . .
4½ " . . . . .
5 .. . . . . .
5½ .. . . . . .
6 " . . . . .
7 " . . . . .
4 " Japanned, .
4½ " " .
5 " " .
5½ " " .
6 " " .
7 " .. .

These Collars form a neat, close-fitting and economical ring for Stove Pipes, holding bright far longer than the zinc.

## TUREEN COVERS.

### LENGTH OF SWELL.

11 inch, . . . .
12 " . . . .
14 " . . . .

## TIN TEA-KETTLE,
## or Coffee-Boiler Bottoms.

### IX TIN.

6 inch sink, . . .
7 " . . .
8 " . . .
9 " . . .

Flanges are 1¼ inches wide.

## SLOP-PAIL FIXTURES.

BREAST, COVER, FOOT.

Cover measured over all.
Breast " " "
Foot " at top.

| Sets. No. | Tin. | Diam. Breast. Inches. | Diam. Foot. Inches. | Diam. Cover. Inches. |
|---|---|---|---|---|
| 100, | IX | 12⅜ | 8¼ | 10 |
| 150, | IC | 12⅜ | 8¼ | 10 |
| 200, | IX | 11⅜ | 7¾ | 9 |
| 250, | IC | 11⅜ | 7¾ | 9 |
| 300, | IX | 10 | 6⅜ | 8 |
| 350, | IC | 10 | 6⅜ | 8 |

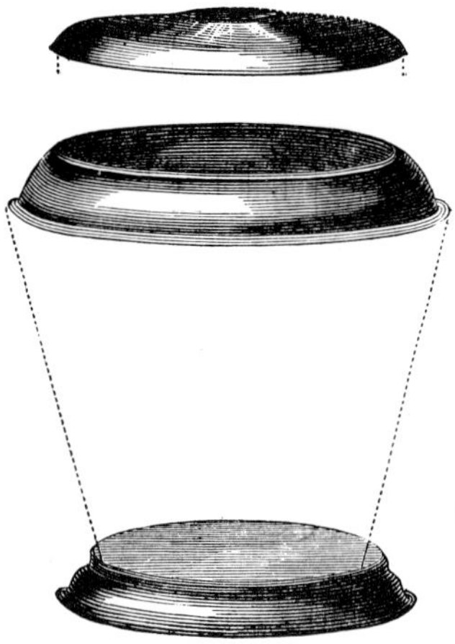

No. 100, Covers, . . .
" 150, " . . .
" 200, " . . .
" 250, " . . .
" 300, " . . .
" 350, " . . .

No. 100, Breasts, . .
" 150, " . .
" 200, " . .
" 250, " . .
" 300, " . .
" 350, " . .

No. 100, Bottom or Foot,
" 150, " "
" 200, " "
" 250, " "
" 300, " "
" 350, " "

These Fixtures constitute nearly all, and the most difficult part of the work in a chamber pail; with these, apprentices or ordinary workmen can manufacture pails rapidly and economically.

## PLATES.

|        |         |       |
|--------|---------|-------|
|        | 5 inch, | . . . |
|        | 6 "     | . . . |
| No. 1  | 7 "     | . . . |
| Extra. | 8 "     | . . . |
|        | 9 "     | . . . |
|        | 10 "    | . . . |

|       |         |       |
|-------|---------|-------|
|       | 9 inch, | . . . |
| No. 2.| 10 "    | . . . |
|       | 11 "    | . . . |

Our No. 1 Extra Plates are made of best charcoal tin; are one inch deep, with imitation wire edges.

## DINING PLATES.

|        |       |             |
|--------|-------|-------------|
| 6 inch,| . . . | . . . . .   |
| 7 "    | . . . | . . . . .   |
| 8 "    | . . . | . . . . .   |
| 9 "    | . . . | . . . . .   |

## BAKER'S PLATES.

|                       |       |
|-----------------------|-------|
| No. 1, $9\frac{1}{2}$ inch, | . . . |
| " 2, $8\frac{1}{2}$ "       | . . . |
| " 3, $7\frac{1}{2}$ "       | . . . |
| " 4, $6\frac{1}{2}$ "       | . . . |

The form of the Baker's Plates is such as to permit the knife, *once drawn across*, to cut the under crust entire.

## SQUASH-PIE PLATES.

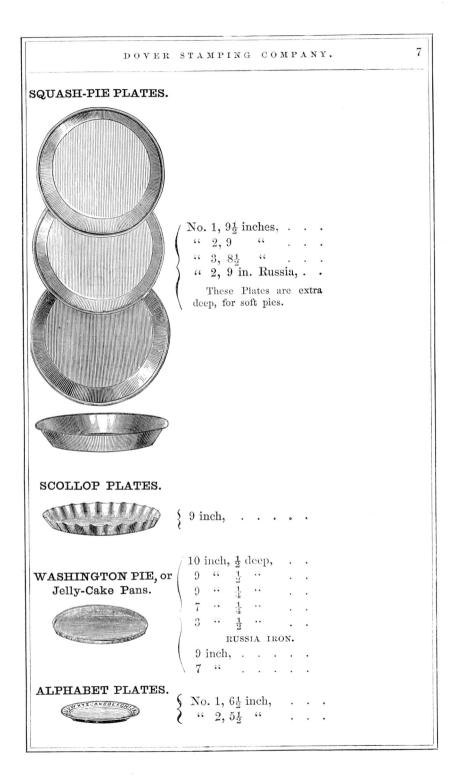

No. 1, 9½ inches, . . .
"  2, 9      "      . . .
"  3, 8½     "      . . .
"  2, 9 in. Russia, . .

These Plates are extra
deep, for soft pies.

## SCOLLOP PLATES.

9 inch, . . . . .

## WASHINGTON PIE, or
## Jelly-Cake Pans.

10 inch, ½ deep, . .
9  "   ½  "   . .
9  "   ¼  "   . .
7  "   ¼  "   . .
3  "   ½  "   . .

RUSSIA IRON.

9 inch, . . . . .
7  "    . . . . .

## ALPHABET PLATES.

No. 1, 6½ inch, . . .
"  2, 5½   "     . . .

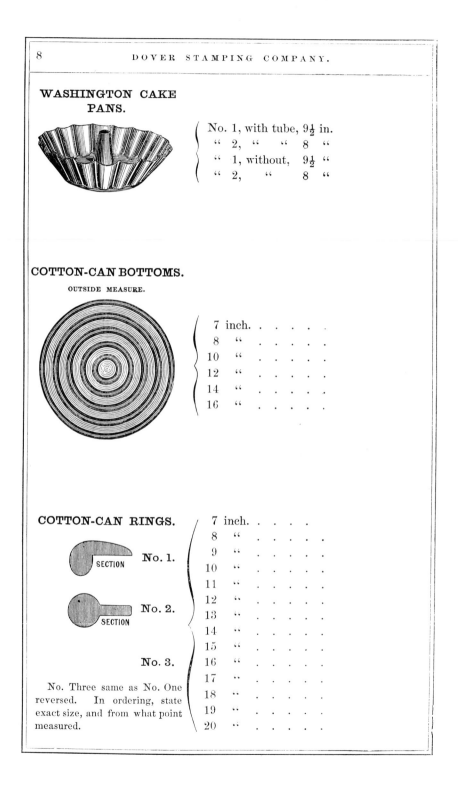

## WASHINGTON CAKE
## PANS.

No. 1, with tube, 9½ in.
" 2, " " 8 "
" 1, without, 9½ "
" 2, " 8 "

## COTTON-CAN BOTTOMS.

OUTSIDE MEASURE.

7 inch. . . . . .
8 " . . . . .
10 " . . . . .
12 " . . . . .
14 " . . . . .
16 " . . . . .

## COTTON-CAN RINGS.

No. 1.

SECTION

No. 2.

SECTION

No. 3.

No. Three same as No. One reversed. In ordering, state exact size, and from what point measured.

7 inch. . . . . .
8 " . . . . .
9 " . . . . .
10 " . . . . .
11 " . . . . .
12 " . . . . .
13 " . . . . .
14 " . . . . .
15 " . . . . .
16 " . . . . .
17 " . . . . .
18 " . . . . .
19 " . . . . .
20 " . . . . .

**WASH BOWL BOTTOMS.**

No. 1, IC, 6¾ inch, . .
" 2, IC, 6¼ " . .
" 1, IX, 6¾ " . .
" 2, IX, 6¼ " . .
Copper, 6¼ " . .

**WASH BOWL FIXTURES.**

HANDLE, TIP, BRACE.

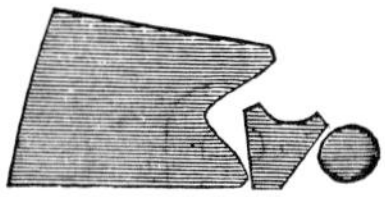

Sets, . . . . . . .

**PAN FEET.**

No. 1, 1 inch, . . . .
" 2, ⅝ " . . . .

**TIPS or CANOPIES.**

No. 1, 1½ inch, . . .
" 2, 1⅜ " . . .
" 3, 1¼ " . . .
" 4, 1⅛ " . . .

**MILK SKIMMERS.**

IX TIN.

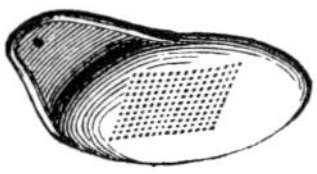

No. 1, Perforated, . .

" 1, Plain, . . . .

**GRATER BLANKS.**

¼ Sheet, . . . . . .
½ " . . . . .
1 " . . . . .

The exact texture, sizes of holes, and distances between them, is shown in the cut.

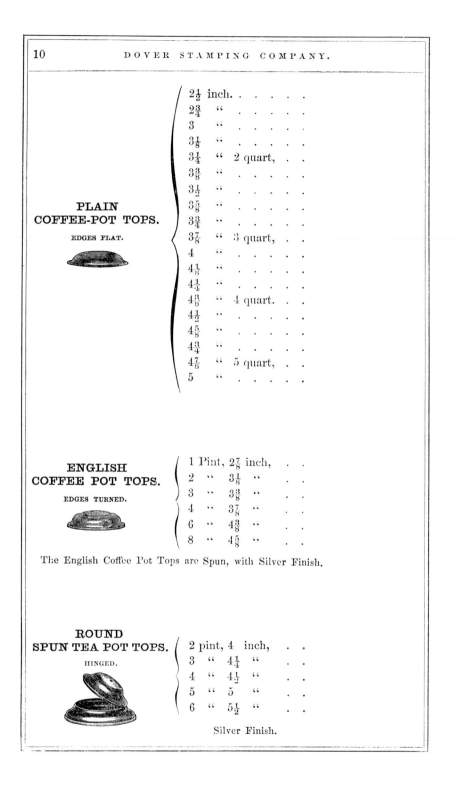

**PLAIN COFFEE-POT TOPS.**

EDGES FLAT.

$2\frac{1}{2}$ inch. . . . . .

$2\frac{3}{4}$ " . . . . .

3 " . . . . .

$3\frac{1}{8}$ " . . . . .

$3\frac{1}{4}$ " 2 quart, . .

$3\frac{3}{8}$ " . . . . .

$3\frac{1}{2}$ " . . . . .

$3\frac{5}{8}$ " . . . . .

$3\frac{3}{4}$ " . . . . .

$3\frac{7}{8}$ " 3 quart, . .

4 " . . . . .

$4\frac{1}{8}$ " . . . . .

$4\frac{1}{4}$ " . . . . .

$4\frac{3}{8}$ " 4 quart. . .

$4\frac{1}{2}$ " . . . . .

$4\frac{5}{8}$ " . . . . .

$4\frac{3}{4}$ " . . . . .

$4\frac{7}{8}$ " 5 quart, . .

5 " . . . . .

**ENGLISH COFFEE POT TOPS.**

EDGES TURNED.

1 Pint, $2\frac{7}{8}$ inch, . .

2 " $3\frac{1}{8}$ " . .

3 " $3\frac{3}{8}$ " . .

4 " $3\frac{7}{8}$ " . .

6 " $4\frac{3}{8}$ " . .

8 " $4\frac{5}{8}$ " . .

The English Coffee Pot Tops are Spun, with Silver Finish.

**ROUND SPUN TEA POT TOPS.**

HINGED.

2 pint, 4 inch, . .

3 " $4\frac{1}{4}$ " . .

4 " $4\frac{1}{2}$ " . .

5 " 5 " . .

6 " $5\frac{1}{2}$ " . .

Silver Finish.

**ROUND
SPUN TEA POT TOPS.**

EDGES TURNED.

| | | |
|---|---|---|
| 2 Pint, | 4 inch, | . . . |
| 3 " | 4¼ " | . . . |
| 4 " | 4½ " | . . . |
| 5 " | 4¾ " | . . . |
| 6 " | 5¼ " | . . . |
| 8 " | 5½ " | . . . |

Silver Finish.

**ROUND PLAIN
TEA POT TOPS.**

EDGES TURNED.

| | | |
|---|---|---|
| 2 Pint, | 4 inch, | . . . |
| 3 " | 4¼ " | . . . |
| 4 " | 4½ " | . . . |
| 5 " | 4¾ " | . . . |
| 6 " | 5¼ " | . . . |
| 8 " | 5½ " | . . . |

**OVAL
TEA POT TOPS.**

PLAIN.

Measure.

| | | |
|---|---|---|
| 2 Pint, | 3¾ x 5⅜ | . . . |
| 3 " | 4¼ x 5¾ | . . . |
| 4 " | 4¾ x 6¼ | . . . |
| 5 " | 5¼ x 6⅝ | . . . |
| 6 " | 5¾ x 7⅛ | . . . |

**OVAL
TEA POT TOPS.**

PLATED.

| | | |
|---|---|---|
| 2 Pint, | 3¾ x 5⅜ in. | . . |
| 3 " | 4¼ x 5¾ " | . . |
| 4 " | 4¾ x 6¼ " | . . |
| 5 " | 5¼ x 6⅝ " | . . |
| 6 " | 5¾ x 7⅛ " | . . |

**OVAL
TEA POT TOPS
AND BOTTOMS.**

WITH HINGES.

| | | |
|---|---|---|
| 2 Pint, | 3¾ x 5⅜ in. | . . |
| 3 " | 4¼ x 5¾ " | . . |
| 4 " | 4¾ x 6¼ " | . . |
| 5 " | 5¼ x 6⅝ " | . . |
| 6 " | 5¾ x 7⅛ " | . . |

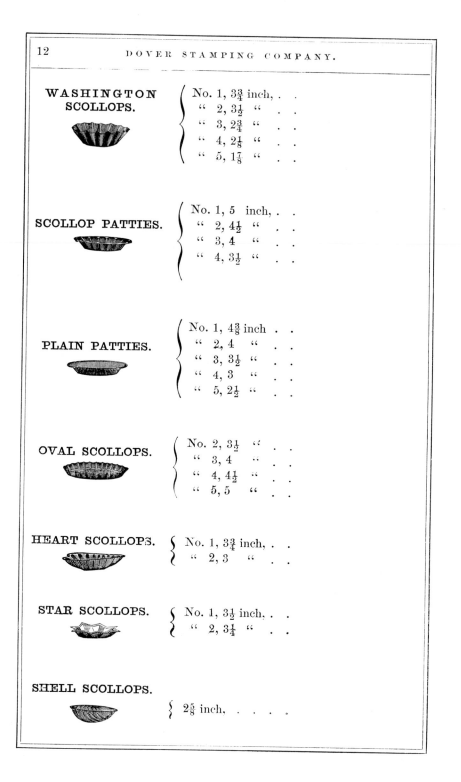

**WASHINGTON SCOLLOPS.**

No. 1, $3\frac{3}{4}$ inch, . .
" 2, $3\frac{1}{2}$ " . .
" 3, $2\frac{3}{4}$ " . .
" 4, $2\frac{1}{8}$ " . .
" 5, $1\frac{7}{8}$ " . .

**SCOLLOP PATTIES.**

No. 1, 5 inch, . .
" 2, $4\frac{1}{2}$ " . .
" 3, 4 " . .
" 4, $3\frac{1}{2}$ " . .

**PLAIN PATTIES.**

No. 1, $4\frac{3}{8}$ inch . .
" 2, 4 " . .
" 3, $3\frac{1}{2}$ " . .
" 4, 3 " . .
" 5, $2\frac{1}{2}$ " . .

**OVAL SCOLLOPS.**

No. 2, $3\frac{1}{2}$ " . .
" 3, 4 " . .
" 4, $4\frac{1}{2}$ " . .
" 5, 5 " . .

**HEART SCOLLOPS.**

No. 1, $3\frac{3}{4}$ inch, . .
" 2, 3 " . .

**STAR SCOLLOPS.**

No. 1, $3\frac{1}{2}$ inch, . .
" 2, $3\frac{1}{4}$ " . .

**SHELL SCOLLOPS.**

$2\frac{5}{8}$ inch, . . . . .

## CANDLE MOULDS.

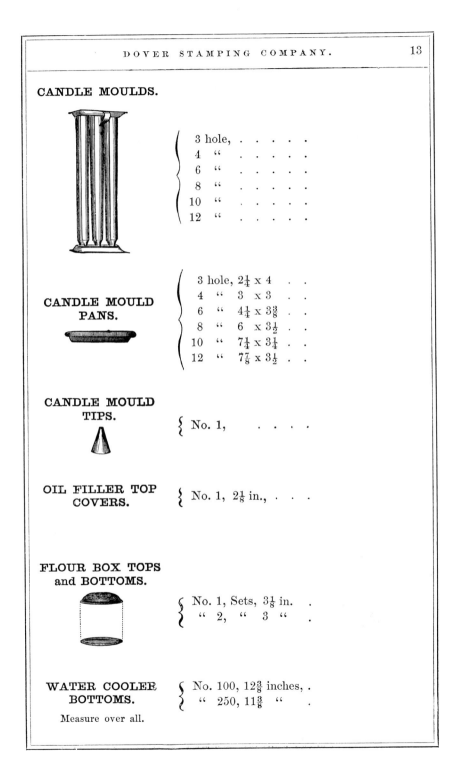

3 hole, . . . . .
4 " . . . . .
6 " . . . . .
8 " . . . . .
10 " . . . . .
12 " . . . . .

## CANDLE MOULD PANS.

3 hole, $2\frac{1}{4}$ x 4 . .
4 " 3 x 3 . .
6 " $4\frac{1}{4}$ x $3\frac{3}{8}$ . .
8 " 6 x $3\frac{1}{2}$ . .
10 " $7\frac{1}{4}$ x $3\frac{1}{4}$ . .
12 " $7\frac{7}{8}$ x $3\frac{1}{2}$ . .

## CANDLE MOULD TIPS.

No. 1, . . . .

## OIL FILLER TOP COVERS.

No. 1, $2\frac{1}{8}$ in., . . .

## FLOUR BOX TOPS and BOTTOMS.

No. 1, Sets, $3\frac{1}{8}$ in. .
" 2, " 3 " .

## WATER COOLER BOTTOMS.

No. 100, $12\frac{3}{8}$ inches, .
" 250, $11\frac{3}{8}$ " .

Measure over all.

## PERFORATED TIN.

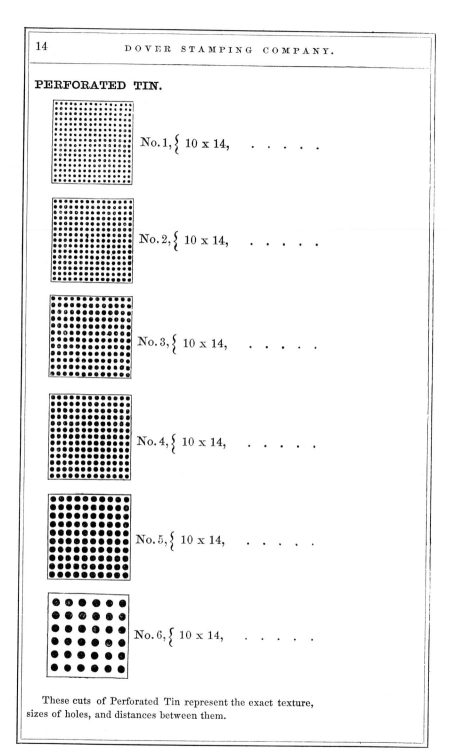

No. 1, $\{$ 10 x 14,   . . . . .

No. 2, $\{$ 10 x 14,   . . . . .

No. 3, $\{$ 10 x 14,   . . . . .

No. 4, $\{$ 10 x 14,   . . . . .

No. 5, $\{$ 10 x 14,   . . . . .

No. 6, $\{$ 10 x 14,   . . . . .

These cuts of Perforated Tin represent the exact texture, sizes of holes, and distances between them.

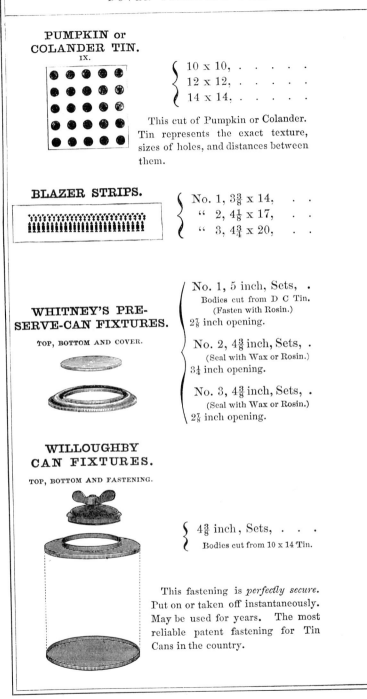

## PUMPKIN or COLANDER TIN.
### IX.

{ 10 x 10, . . . . .
12 x 12, . . . . .
14 x 14, . . . . .

This cut of Pumpkin or Colander. Tin represents the exact texture, sizes of holes, and distances between them.

## BLAZER STRIPS.

{ No. 1, $3\frac{3}{8}$ x 14, . .
" 2, $4\frac{1}{8}$ x 17, . .
" 3, $4\frac{3}{4}$ x 20, . .

## WHITNEY'S PRE-SERVE-CAN FIXTURES.

TOP, BOTTOM AND COVER.

No. 1, 5 inch, Sets, .
Bodies cut from D C Tin.
(Fasten with Rosin.)
$2\frac{7}{8}$ inch opening.

No. 2, $4\frac{3}{8}$ inch, Sets, .
(Seal with Wax or Rosin.)
$3\frac{1}{4}$ inch opening.

No. 3, $4\frac{3}{8}$ inch, Sets, .
(Seal with Wax or Rosin.)
$2\frac{7}{8}$ inch opening.

## WILLOUGHBY CAN FIXTURES.

TOP, BOTTOM AND FASTENING.

{ $4\frac{3}{8}$ inch, Sets, . . .
Bodies cut from 10 x 14 Tin.

This fastening is *perfectly secure.* Put on or taken off instantaneously. May be used for years. The most reliable patent fastening for Tin Cans in the country.

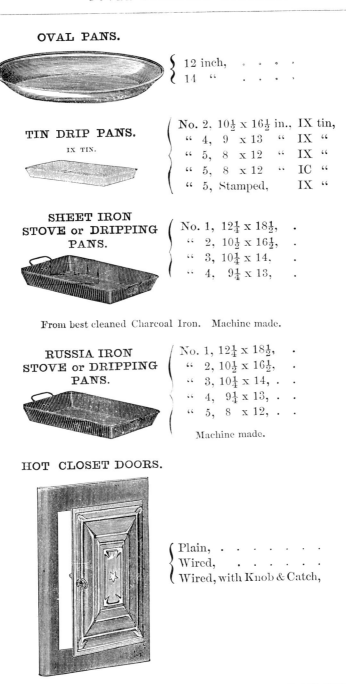

## OVAL PANS.

{ 12 inch, . . . .
{ 14 " . . . .

**TIN DRIP PANS.**

IX TIN.

{ No. 2, 10½ x 16½ in., IX tin,
{ " 4, 9 x 13 " IX "
{ " 5, 8 x 12 " IX "
{ " 5, 8 x 12 " IC "
{ " 5, Stamped, IX "

**SHEET IRON**
**STOVE or DRIPPING**
**PANS.**

{ No. 1, 12¼ x 18½, .
{ " 2, 10½ x 16½, .
{ " 3, 10¼ x 14, .
{ " 4, 9¼ x 13, .

From best cleaned Charcoal Iron. Machine made.

**RUSSIA IRON**
**STOVE or DRIPPING**
**PANS.**

{ No. 1, 12¼ x 18½, .
{ " 2, 10½ x 16½, .
{ " 3, 10¼ x 14, . .
{ " 4, 9¼ x 13, . .
{ " 5, 8 x 12, . .

Machine made.

## HOT CLOSET DOORS.

{ Plain, . . . . . .
{ Wired, . . . . . .
{ Wired, with Knob & Catch,

## WASH BOILER COVERS.

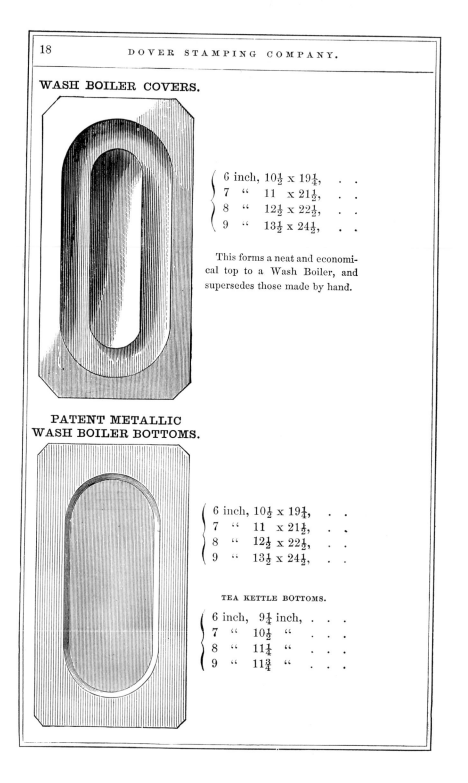

$\left\{\begin{array}{l} \text{6 inch, } 10\frac{1}{2} \times 19\frac{1}{4}, \quad . \quad . \\ \text{7 " } \quad 11 \ \times 21\frac{1}{2}, \quad . \quad . \\ \text{8 " } \quad 12\frac{1}{2} \times 22\frac{1}{2}, \quad . \quad . \\ \text{9 " } \quad 13\frac{1}{2} \times 24\frac{1}{2}, \quad . \quad . \end{array}\right.$

This forms a neat and economical top to a Wash Boiler, and supersedes those made by hand.

## PATENT METALLIC
## WASH BOILER BOTTOMS.

$\left\{\begin{array}{l} \text{6 inch, } 10\frac{1}{2} \times 19\frac{1}{4}, \quad . \quad . \\ \text{7 " } \quad 11 \ \times 21\frac{1}{2}, \quad . \quad . \\ \text{8 " } \quad 12\frac{1}{2} \times 22\frac{1}{2}, \quad . \quad . \\ \text{9 " } \quad 13\frac{1}{2} \times 24\frac{1}{2}, \quad . \quad . \end{array}\right.$

#### TEA KETTLE BOTTOMS.

$\left\{\begin{array}{l} \text{6 inch, } 9\frac{1}{4} \text{ inch, } . \quad . \quad . \\ \text{7 " } \quad 10\frac{1}{2} \text{ " } \quad . \quad . \quad . \\ \text{8 " } \quad 11\frac{1}{4} \text{ " } \quad . \quad . \quad . \\ \text{9 " } \quad 11\frac{3}{4} \text{ " } \quad . \quad . \quad . \end{array}\right.$

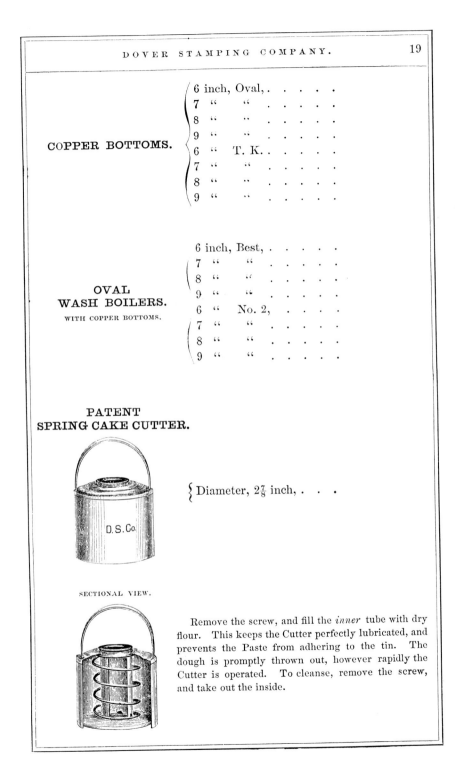

COPPER BOTTOMS.

6 inch, Oval, . . . . .
7 " " . . . . .
8 " " . . . . .
9 " " . . . . .
6 " T. K.. . . . .
7 " " . . . . .
8 " " . . . . .
9 " " . . . . .

OVAL
WASH BOILERS.
WITH COPPER BOTTOMS.

6 inch, Best, . . . . .
7 " " . . . . .
8 " " . . . . .
9 " " . . . . .
6 " No. 2, . . . .
7 " " . . . . .
8 " " . . . . .
9 " " . . . . .

PATENT
SPRING CAKE CUTTER.

D. S. Co.

{ Diameter, $2\frac{7}{8}$ inch, . . .

SECTIONAL VIEW.

Remove the screw, and fill the *inner* tube with dry flour. This keeps the Cutter perfectly lubricated, and prevents the Paste from adhering to the tin. The dough is promptly thrown out, however rapidly the Cutter is operated. To cleanse, remove the screw, and take out the inside.

## CAKE CUTTERS.

No. 1,    .   .   .   .   .   .

"  2,    .   .   .   .   .   .

"  3,    .   .   .   .   .   .

The cut represents No. 2.
No. 1 has more, and No. 3 less
fancy filling.  Each dozen has
the variety represented.

## OAK LEAF
## CAKE CUTTERS.

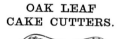

No. 1,    .   .   .   .   .   .

"  2,    .   .   .   .   .   .

"  3,    .   .   .   .   .   .

These are not assorted.

## DOUGHNUT CUTTER.

{ 3 inch,    .   .   .   .   .   .

## GRAVY STRAINERS.

No. 1,    .   .   .   .   .   .

"  2,    .   .   .   .   .   .

"  3,    .   .   .   .   .   .

Extra well made.   Concave
bottoms.   Foot hemmed, ex-
cept on No. 3.

## GRAVY STRAINERS.

BLACK WOOD HANDLE.

{ No. 10,    .   .   .   .   .   .

"  20,    .   .   .   .   .   .

## VEGETABLE GRATERS.

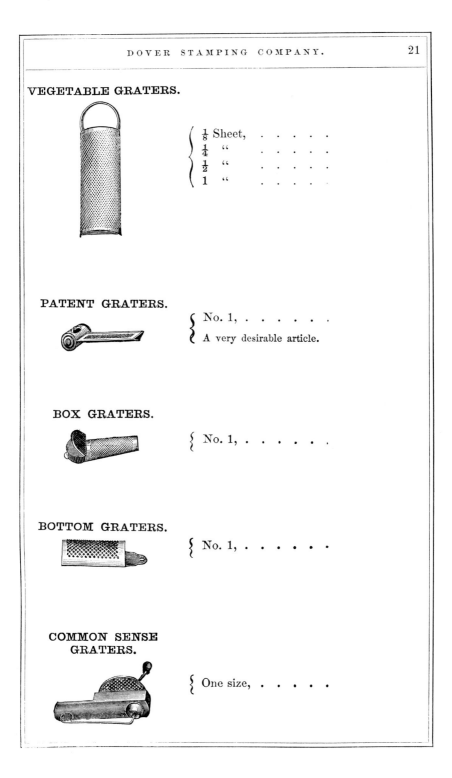

$\frac{1}{8}$ Sheet, . . . . .
$\frac{1}{4}$ " . . . .
$\frac{1}{2}$ " . . . .
1 " . . . .

## PATENT GRATERS.

No. 1, . . . . . .
A very desirable article.

## BOX GRATERS.

No. 1, . . . . . .

## BOTTOM GRATERS.

No. 1, . . . . . .

## COMMON SENSE GRATERS.

One size, . . . . .

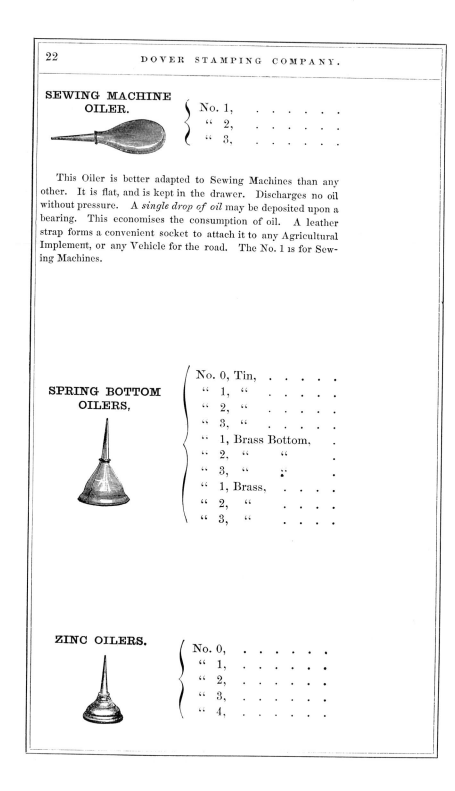

## SEWING MACHINE OILER.

No. 1,  . . . . . .
" 2,  . . . . .
" 3,  . . . . . .

This Oiler is better adapted to Sewing Machines than any other. It is flat, and is kept in the drawer. Discharges no oil without pressure. A *single drop of oil* may be deposited upon a bearing. This economises the consumption of oil. A leather strap forms a convenient socket to attach it to any Agricultural Implement, or any Vehicle for the road. The No. 1 is for Sewing Machines.

## SPRING BOTTOM OILERS,

No. 0, Tin,  . . . . .
" 1, "  . . . . .
" 2, "  . . . . .
" 3, "  . . . . .
" 1, Brass Bottom,  .
" 2, "  "  .
" 3, "  ..  .
" 1, Brass,  . . . .
" 2, "  . . . .
" 3, "  . . . .

## ZINC OILERS.

No. 0,  . . . . . .
" 1,  . . . . . .
" 2,  . . . . . .
" 3,  . . . . . .
" 4,  . . . . . .

## SPRING TOP OILERS.

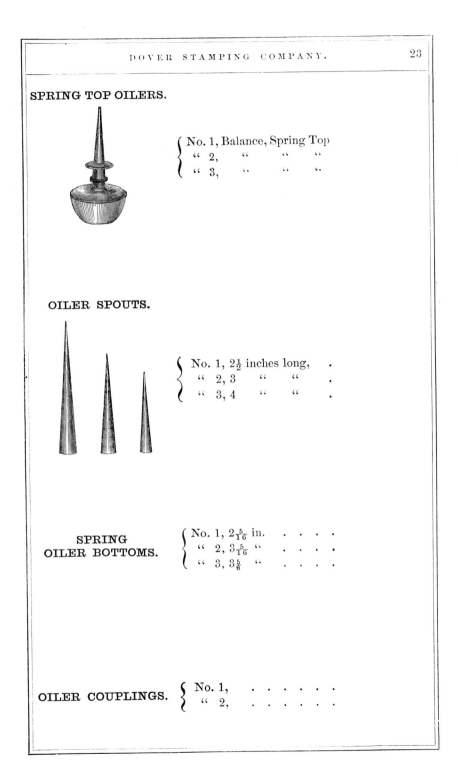

$\left\{\begin{array}{l}\text{No. 1, Balance, Spring Top} \\ \text{`` 2, `` `` ``} \\ \text{`` 3, `` `` ``}\end{array}\right.$

## OILER SPOUTS.

$\left\{\begin{array}{l}\text{No. 1, } 2\frac{1}{2} \text{ inches long, } \quad . \\ \text{`` 2, 3 `` `` } \quad . \\ \text{`` 3, 4 `` `` } \quad .\end{array}\right.$

## SPRING OILER BOTTOMS.

$\left\{\begin{array}{l}\text{No. 1, } 2\frac{5}{16} \text{ in.} \quad . \quad . \quad . \\ \text{`` 2, } 3\frac{5}{16} \text{ `` } \quad . \quad . \quad . \\ \text{`` 3, } 3\frac{5}{8} \text{ `` } \quad . \quad . \quad . \end{array}\right.$

## OILER COUPLINGS.

$\left\{\begin{array}{l}\text{No. 1, } \quad . \quad . \quad . \quad . \quad . \\ \text{`` 2, } \quad . \quad . \quad . \quad . \quad . \end{array}\right.$

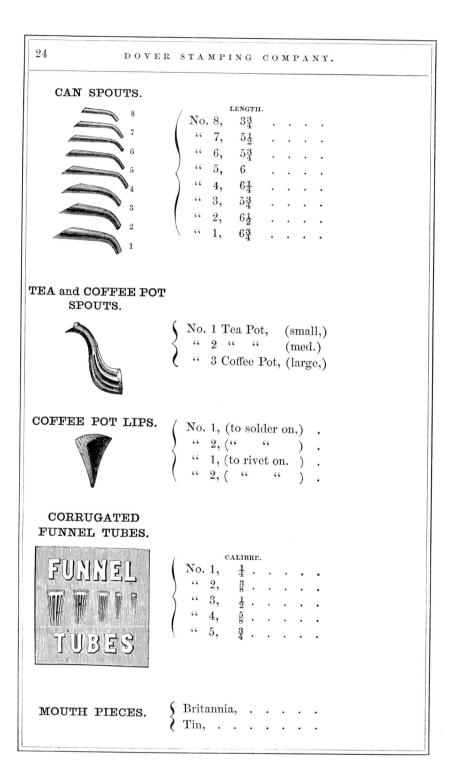

## CAN SPOUTS.

LENGTH.

No. 8,   $3\frac{3}{4}$   . . . .
"   7,   $5\frac{1}{2}$   . . . .
"   6,   $5\frac{3}{4}$   . . . .
"   5,   6   . . . .
"   4,   $6\frac{1}{4}$   . . . .
"   3,   $5\frac{3}{4}$   . . . .
"   2,   $6\frac{1}{2}$   . . . .
"   1,   $6\frac{3}{4}$   . . . .

## TEA and COFFEE POT SPOUTS.

No. 1 Tea Pot,   (small,)
"   2   "   "   (med.)
"   3 Coffee Pot, (large,)

## COFFEE POT LIPS.

No. 1, (to solder on,)   .
"   2, ("   "   )   .
"   1, (to rivet on.   )   .
"   2, (   "   "   )   .

## CORRUGATED FUNNEL TUBES.

CALIBRE.

No. 1,   $\frac{1}{4}$ . . . . .
"   2,   $\frac{3}{8}$ . . . . .
"   3,   $\frac{1}{2}$ . . . . .
"   4,   $\frac{5}{8}$ . . . . .
"   5,   $\frac{3}{4}$ . . . . .

## MOUTH PIECES.

Britannia, . . . . .
Tin, . . . . . . .

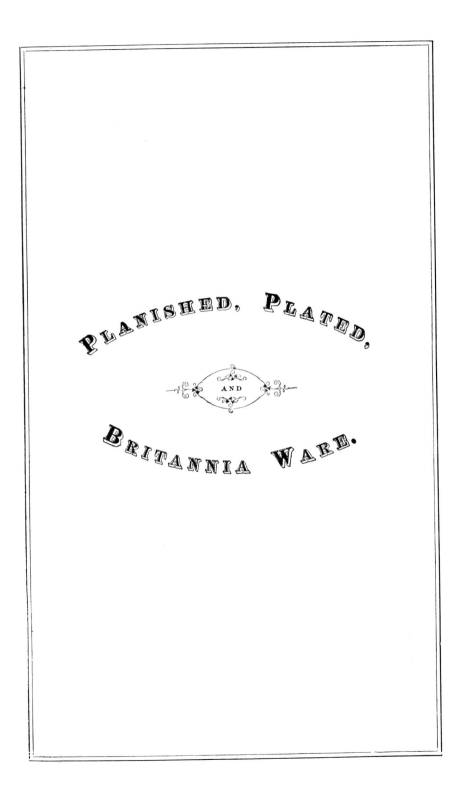

PLANISHED, PLATED,

AND

BRITANNIA WARE.

# TOBACCO BOXES.

### SILVER FINISH.

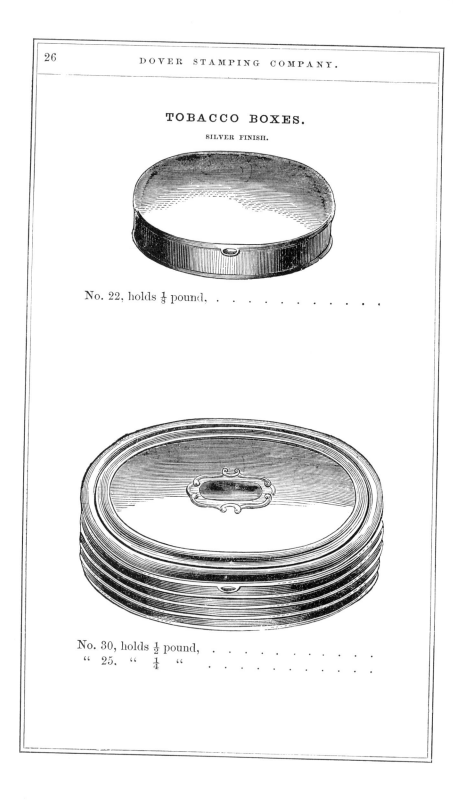

No. 22, holds ⅛ pound, . . . . . . . . . .

No. 30, holds ½ pound, . . . . . . . . . . .
" 25, " ¼ " . . . . . . . . . .

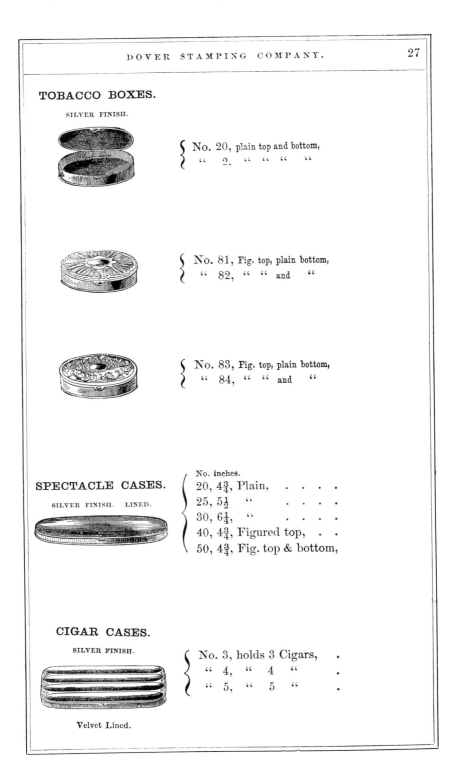

## TOBACCO BOXES.

SILVER FINISH.

{ No. 20, plain top and bottom,
  " 2, " " " "

{ No. 81, Fig. top, plain bottom,
  " 82, " " and "

{ No. 83, Fig. top, plain bottom,
  " 84, " " and "

## SPECTACLE CASES.

SILVER FINISH. LINED.

{ No. inches.
  20, 4¾, Plain, . . . .
  25, 5½, " . . . .
  30, 6¼, " . . . .
  40, 4¾, Figured top, . .
  50, 4¾, Fig. top & bottom,

## CIGAR CASES.

SILVER FINISH.

{ No. 3, holds 3 Cigars, .
  " 4, " 4 " .
  " 5, " 5 " .

Velvet Lined.

## OYSTER BLAZERS.

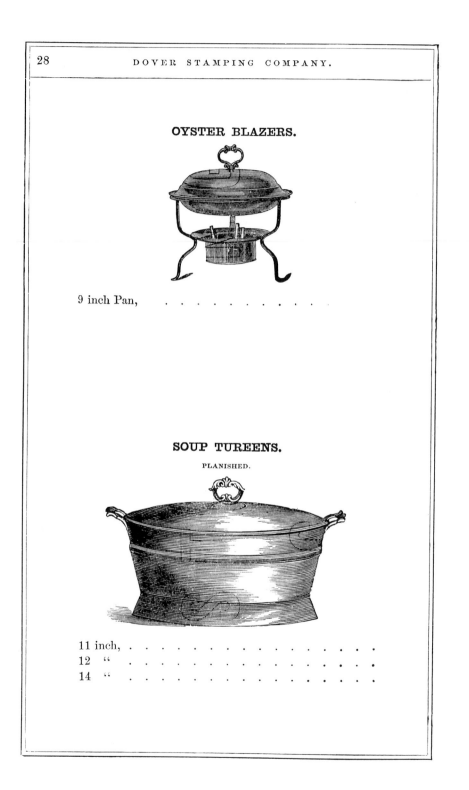

9 inch Pan,    .    .    .    .    .    .    .    .    .    .

## SOUP TUREENS.

### PLANISHED.

11 inch, .    .    .    .    .    .    .    .    .    .    .    .    .
12  "    .    .    .    .    .    .    .    .    .    .    .    .    .
14  "    .    .    .    .    .    .    .    .    .    .    .    .    .

## JELLY MOULDS.

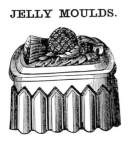

½ Pint, . . . . .
1 " . . . . .
1½ " . . . . .
2 " . . . . .
½ Pint, with Rim, . .
1 " " " . . .
1½ " " " . . .
2 " " " . . .

Ornamented with Sheafs of
Wheat, Corn, Lilly, Grapes, &c.

## MELON MOULDS.

LENGTH.

No. 3, 6½ inches, . . .
" 4, 7¼ " . . .
" 5, 8 " . . .
" 6, 8½ " . . .
" 7, 9 " . . .

## ICE CREAM MOULDS.

2 Pint, . . . . . .
3 " . . . . . .
4 " . . . . . .
5 " . . . . . .
6 " . . . . . .
7 " . . . . . .

## PLANISHED TIN TEA POTS.

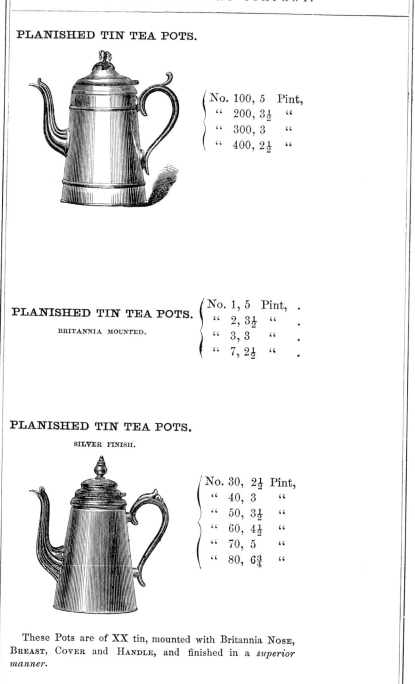

No. 100, 5  Pint,
"  200, 3½  "
"  300, 3   "
"  400, 2½  "

### PLANISHED TIN TEA POTS.

BRITANNIA MOUNTED.

No. 1, 5  Pint,  .
"  2, 3½  "  .
"  3, 3   "  .
"  7, 2½  "  .

## PLANISHED TIN TEA POTS.

SILVER FINISH.

No. 30, 2½ Pint,
"  40, 3   "
"  50, 3½  "
"  60, 4½  "
"  70, 5   "
"  80, 6¾  "

These Pots are of **XX** tin, mounted with Britannia Nose, Breast, Cover and Handle, and finished in a *superior manner.*

## CLARIFYING COFFEE STEEPER.

PLANISHED.

No. 4, 1½ Quarts, .
" 3, 2¼ " .
" 2, 3 "
" 1, 4 "

The construction of this Steeper is such as to retain all the aroma within the Pot. The product is "French Boiled Coffee."

## PLANISHED TIN COFFEE POTS.

BRITANNIA MOUNTED.

No. 1, 4 Quarts,
" 2, 3½ "
" 3, 2½ "
" 4, 2 "

## NOVELTY COFFEE POT.

2 Quarts, . . . . .
3   " . . . .
4   " . . . .
5   " . . . .
6   " . . . .

## FIRE PROOF POTS.

700, . . . . .
710, . . . . .
720, . . . . .
730, . . . . .
740, . . . . .

Planished Tin Bodies,
with Fire Proof Bottoms.

## BRITANNIA POTS.

FIRE PROOF.

1200, . . . . .
1210, . . . . .
1220, . . . . .
1230, . . . . .
1240, . . . . .

## BRITANNIA POTS.

FIRE PROOF.

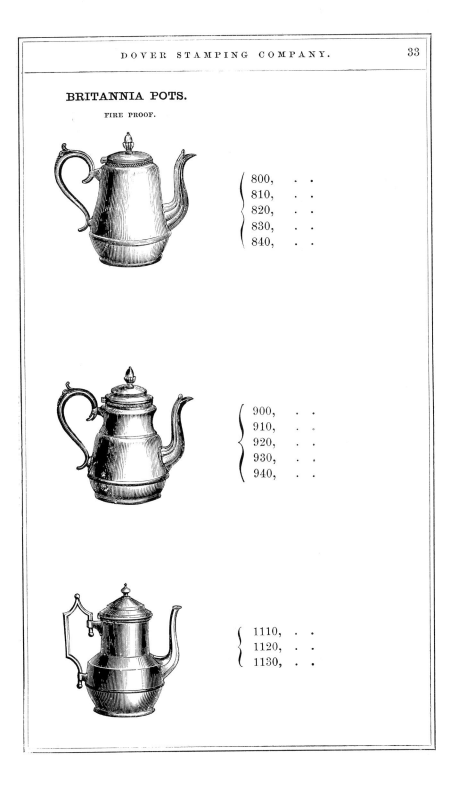

800, · ·
810, · ·
820, · ·
830, · ·
840, · ·

900, · ·
910, · ∘
920, · ·
930, · ∘
940, · ·

1110, · ·
1120, · ·
1130, · ·

**BRITANNIA.**

No. 5, . . . . . .

No. 4, similar to No. 2,
   " 9,    "    "    2,

**BRITANNIA.**

No. 2, . . . . . .

**BRITANNIA.**

WITH COPPER BOTTOMS.

No. 04,    . . . . .
   " 05,    . . . . .
   " 4½,    . . . . .
   " 5½,    . . . . .
   " 3, Coffee,    . . .

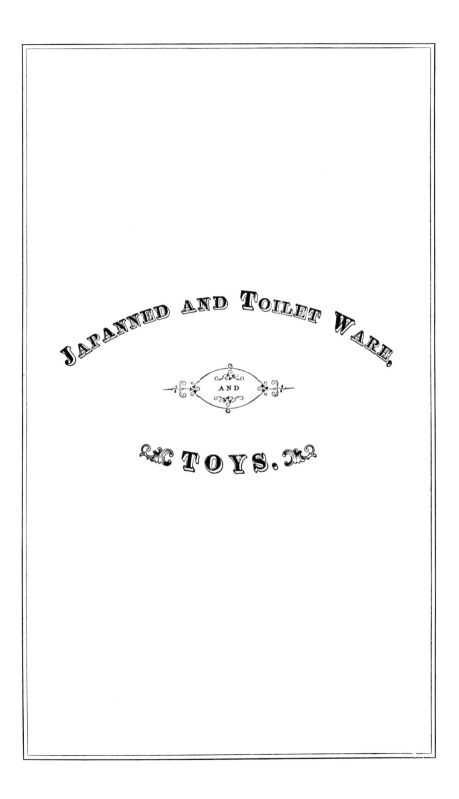

JAPANNED AND TOILET WARE,

AND

TOYS.

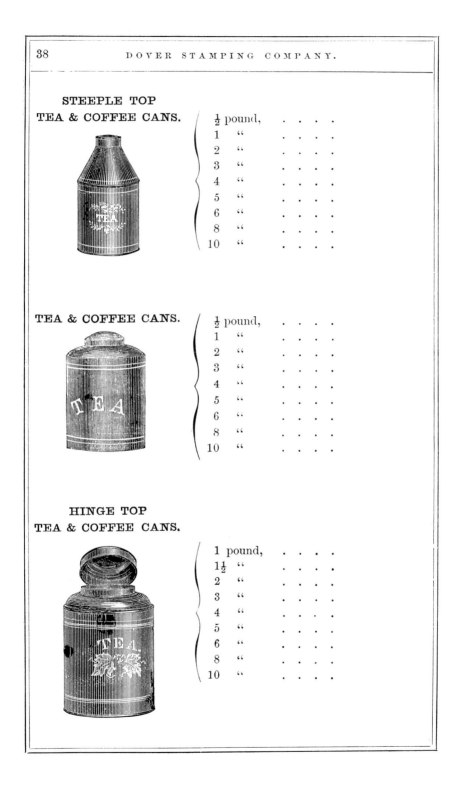

**STEEPLE TOP
TEA & COFFEE CANS.**

½ pound, . . . .
1 " . . . .
2 " . . . .
3 " . . . .
4 " . . . .
5 " . . . .
6 " . . . .
8 " . . . .
10 " . . . .

**TEA & COFFEE CANS.**

½ pound, . . . .
1 " . . . .
2 " . . . .
3 " . . . .
4 " . . . .
5 " . . . .
6 " . . . .
8 " . . . .
10 " . . . .

**HINGE TOP
TEA & COFFEE CANS.**

1 pound, . . . .
1½ " . . . .
2 " . . . .
3 " . . . .
4 " . . . .
5 " . . . .
6 " . . . .
8 " . . . .
10 " . . . .

## SUGAR BOXES.

No. 1,   5 in. diameter,   .   .
"   2,   6   "      "      .
"   3,   6¾   "      "      .
"   4,   7½   "      "      .
"   5,   8   "      "      .
"   6,   10¼   "      "      .
"   7,   11   "      "      .
"   8,   12   "      "      .
"   9,   12½   "      "      .

In nests of 4,
"     "     5,
"     "     8,
"     "     9

## TRUNKS.

LARGEST 9¼ INCHES.

Nests of 2, wire handle,   .   .
"      3,    "      "      .
"      4,    "      "      .
"      5,    "      "      .

Nests of 4, brass handle,
"      5,    "      "
"      7,    "      "

## CAMBRIDGE
## SPICE BOX.

6 Round Boxes inside,   .   .

## ROUND SPICE BOXES.

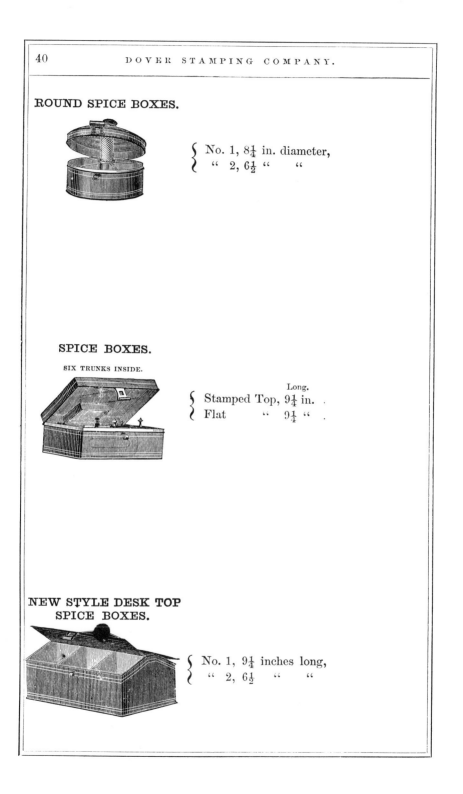

⎰ No. 1, 8¼ in. diameter,
⎱ " 2, 6½ "    "

## SPICE BOXES.

SIX TRUNKS INSIDE.

Long.

⎰ Stamped Top, 9¼ in.  .
⎱ Flat        " 9¼ "  .

## NEW STYLE DESK TOP
## SPICE BOXES.

⎰ No. 1, 9¼ inches long,
⎱ " 2, 6½   "     "

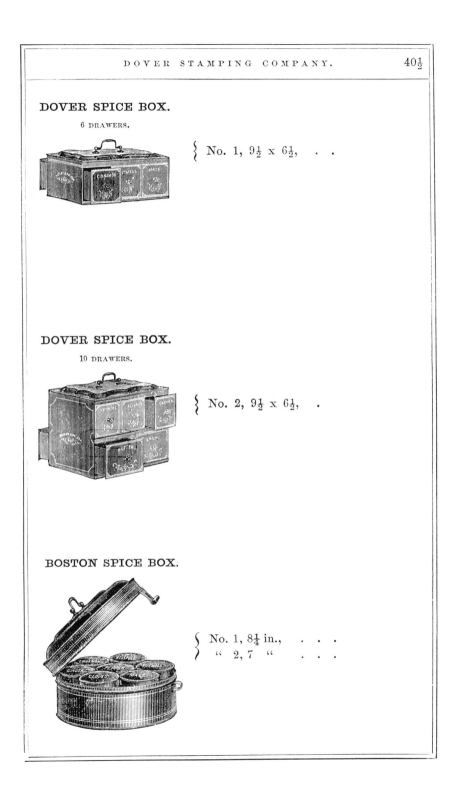

## DOVER SPICE BOX.

6 DRAWERS.

{ No. 1, 9½ x 6½, . .

## DOVER SPICE BOX.

10 DRAWERS.

{ No. 2, 9½ x 6½, . 

## BOSTON SPICE BOX.

{ No. 1, 8¼ in., . . .
{ " 2, 7 " . . .

**SQUARE CAKE or BREAD BOXES.**

No. Long.    Deep.    Thick.
1,  12  x  8½ x  8¼,  .
2,  13½ x  9  x  9¼,  .
3,  14¼ x 10¼ x 10,   .
4,  15½ x 11  x 11¼,  .
5,  16¾ x 11¾ x 12,   .
6,  18  x 12½ x 13,   .

Nests of 3, first 3 sizes,
"    "  4, "    4  "
"    "  5, "    5  "
"    "  6, "    6  "

**ROUND CAKE BOXES.**

No. 1, 10 in. diameter
"   2, 11  "        "
"   3, 12  "        "
In nests of 3, per nest,

## FORK AND SPOON BOXES.

FLANNEL LINED.

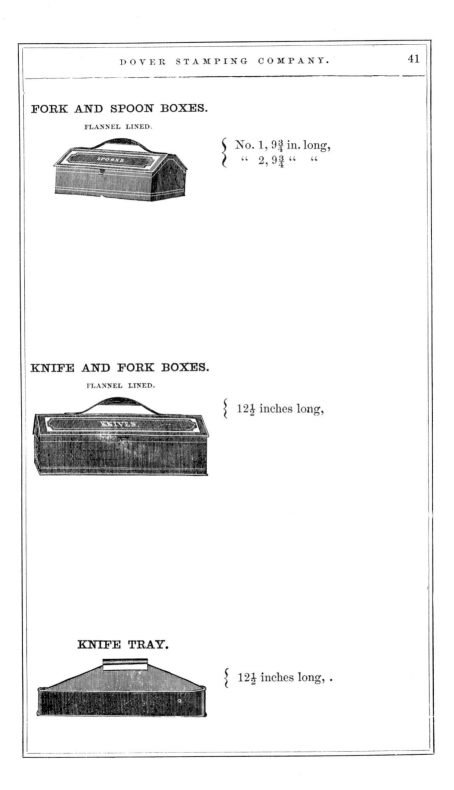

No. 1, 9¾ in. long,
" 2, 9¾ " "

## KNIFE AND FORK BOXES.

FLANNEL LINED.

12½ inches long,

## KNIFE TRAY.

12½ inches long, .

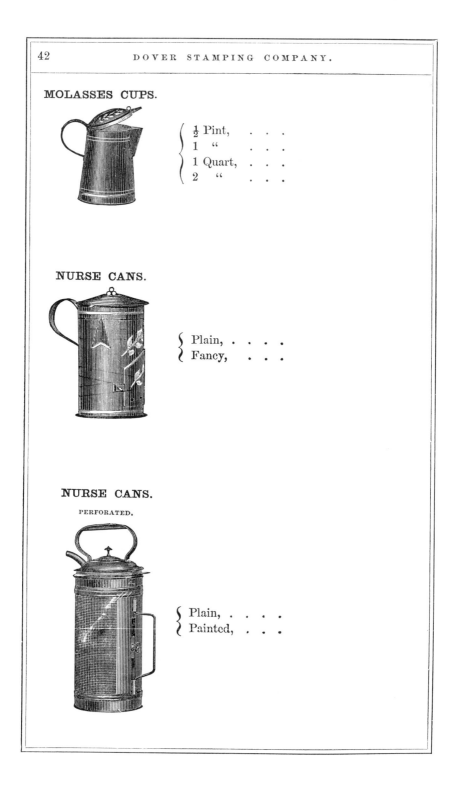

## MOLASSES CUPS.

½ Pint,    . . .
1   "      . . .
1 Quart,   . . .
2   "      . . .

## NURSE CANS.

Plain, . . . .
Fancy,   . . .

## NURSE CANS.

PERFORATED.

Plain, . . . .
Painted,  . . .

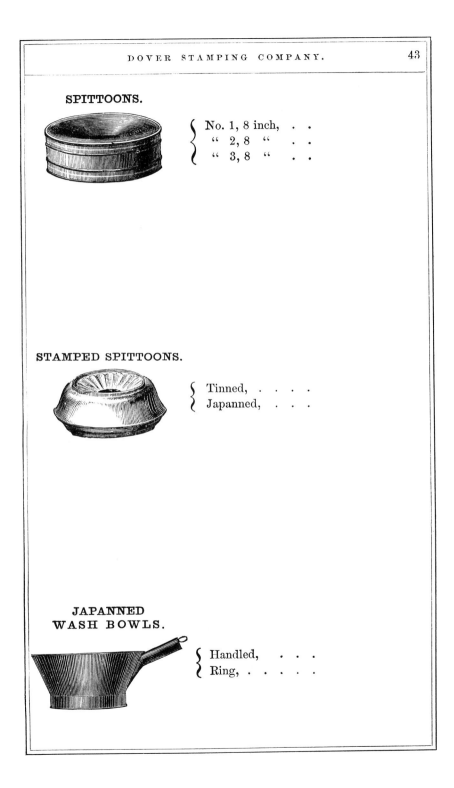

## SPITTOONS.

{ No. 1, 8 inch, . .
" 2, 8 " . .
" 3, 8 " . .

## STAMPED SPITTOONS.

{ Tinned, . . . .
Japanned, . . .

## JAPANNED
## WASH BOWLS.

{ Handled, . . .
Ring, . . . . .

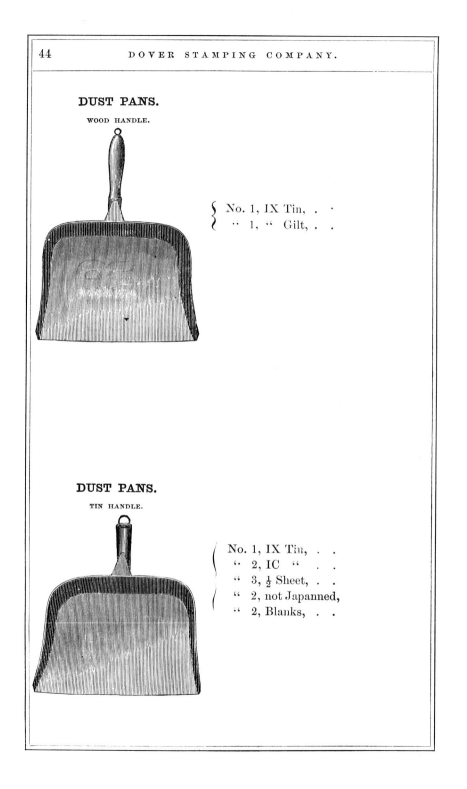

## DUST PANS.

WOOD HANDLE.

No. 1, IX Tin, . ·
" 1, " Gilt, . .

## DUST PANS.

TIN HANDLE.

No. 1, IX Tin, . .
" 2, IC " . .
" 3, ½ Sheet, . .
" 2, not Japanned,
" 2, Blanks, . .

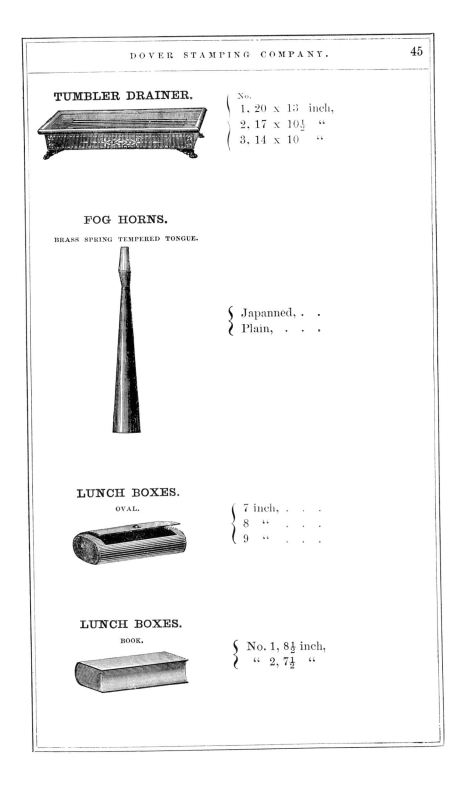

## TUMBLER DRAINER.

No.
1. 20 x 13 inch,
2. 17 x 10½ "
3. 14 x 10 "

## FOG HORNS.

BRASS SPRING TEMPERED TONGUE.

Japanned, . . .
Plain, . . . .

## LUNCH BOXES.

OVAL.

7 inch, . . .
8 " . . .
9 " . . .

## LUNCH BOXES.

BOOK.

No. 1, 8½ inch,
" 2, 7½ "

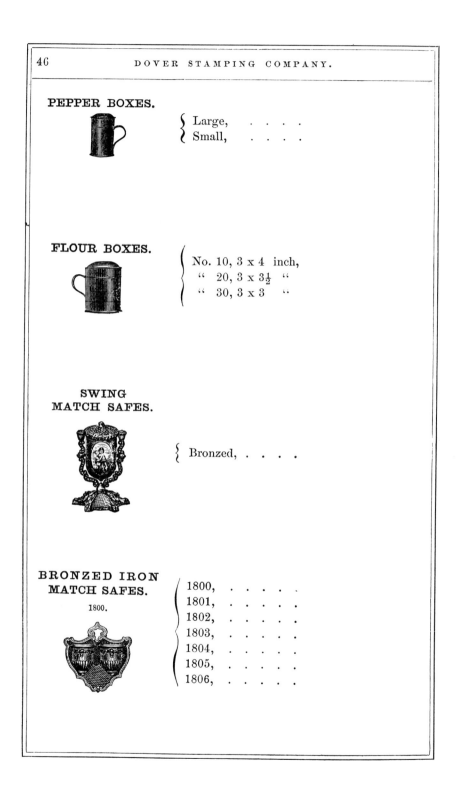

**PEPPER BOXES.**

$\left\{\begin{array}{l}\end{array}\right.$ Large,    .   .   .   .
      Small,    .   .   .   .

**FLOUR BOXES.**

$\left\{\begin{array}{l}\end{array}\right.$ No. 10, 3 x 4   inch,
     "   20, 3 x 3½   "
     "   30, 3 x 3    "

**SWING
MATCH SAFES.**

$\left\{\begin{array}{l}\end{array}\right.$ Bronzed,   .   .   .   .

**BRONZED IRON
MATCH SAFES.**

1800.

$\left\{\begin{array}{l}\end{array}\right.$ 1800,   .   .   .   .
     1801,   .   .   .   .
     1802,   .   .   .   .
     1803,   .   .   .   .
     1804,   .   .   .   .
     1805,   .   .   .   .
     1806,   .   .   .   .

## PATENT SPRING
## MATCH SAFES.

SELF CLOSING.

Different colors, . . .

The most convenient article in the market. Excludes moisture and mice. Always closed.

## MATCH SAFES.

SQUARE.

No. 1, 4 inches long, .
" 2, 3 " " .
Round, . . . . .

## MATCH SAFES.

TWIN.

No. 1, . . . .

## POCKET
## MATCH SAFES.

SILVER FINISH.

No. 1, . . . . .
" 2, . . . . .

IRON MATCH SAFES.

No. 0, Black, Plain, .
" 1, " " .
" 2, " " .
" 10, Fancy Finish,
" 11, " "
" 12, " "

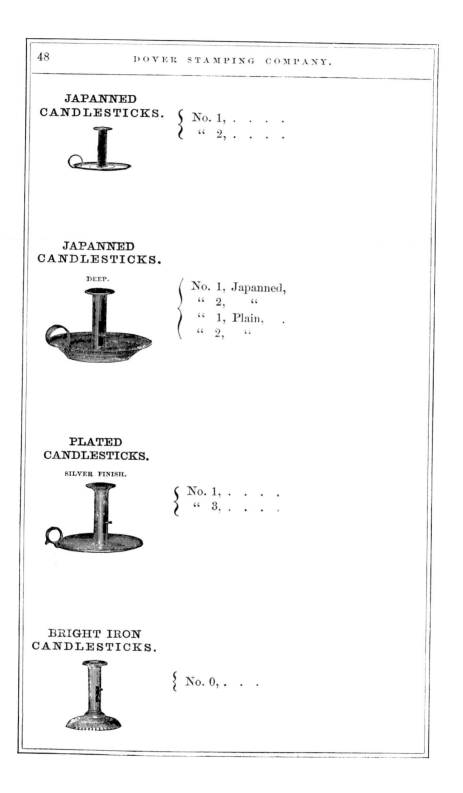

**JAPANNED
CANDLESTICKS.**

No. 1, . . . .
" 2, . . . .

**JAPANNED
CANDLESTICKS.**

DEEP.

No. 1, Japanned,
" 2, "
" 1, Plain, .
" 2, "

**PLATED
CANDLESTICKS.**

SILVER FINISH.

No. 1, . . . .
" 3, . . . .

**BRIGHT IRON
CANDLESTICKS.**

No. 0, . . .

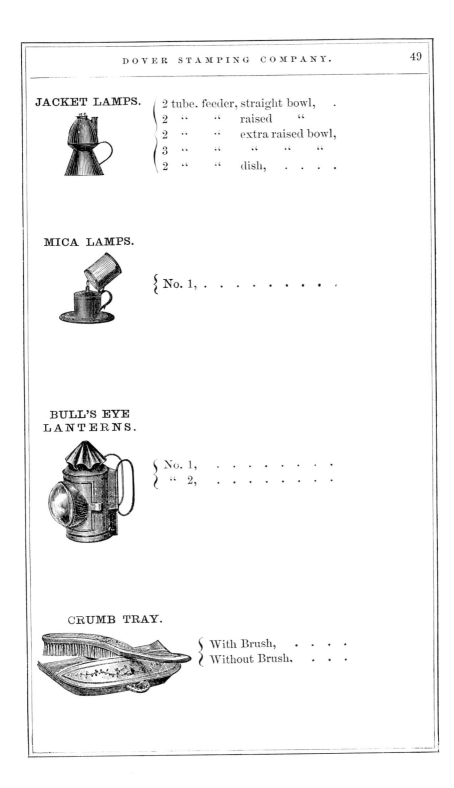

**JACKET LAMPS.**

2 tube. feeder, straight bowl, .
2 " " raised "
2 " " extra raised bowl,
3 " " " " "
2 " " dish, . . . .

**MICA LAMPS.**

No. 1, . . . . . . . . .

**BULL'S EYE LANTERNS.**

No. 1, . . . . . . .
" 2, . . . . . . .

**CRUMB TRAY.**

With Brush, . . . .
Without Brush. . . .

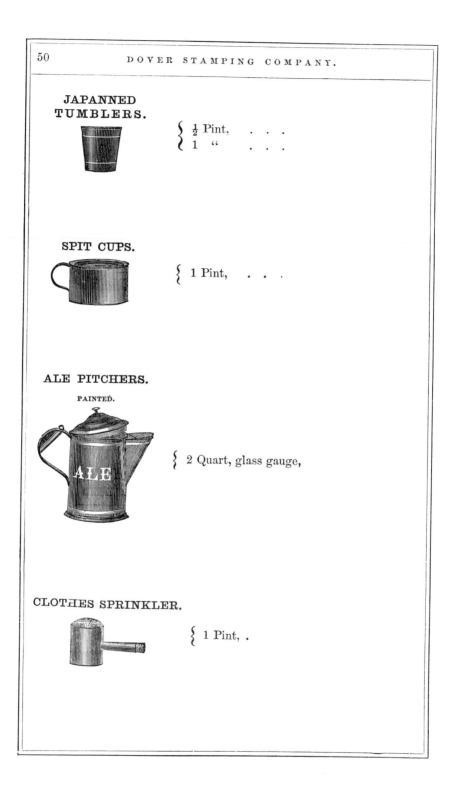

**JAPANNED
TUMBLERS.**

$\frac{1}{2}$ Pint,   .   .   .
1 "     .   .   .

**SPIT CUPS.**

1 Pint,   .   .   .

**ALE PITCHERS.**

PAINTED.

2 Quart, glass gauge,

**CLOTHES SPRINKLER.**

1 Pint, .

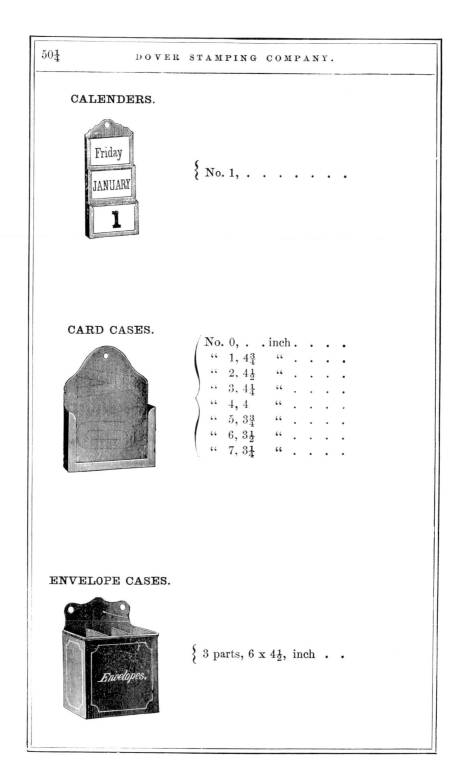

## CALENDERS.

{ No. 1, . . . . . . .

## CARD CASES.

No. 0, . . inch . . . .
" 1, $4\frac{3}{4}$   " . . . .
" 2, $4\frac{1}{2}$   " . . . .
" 3, $4\frac{1}{4}$   " . . . .
" 4, 4   " . . . .
" 5, $3\frac{3}{4}$   " . . . .
" 6, $3\frac{1}{2}$   " . . . .
" 7, $3\frac{1}{4}$   " . . . .

## ENVELOPE CASES.

{ 3 parts, 6 x $4\frac{1}{2}$, inch . .

**ENVELOPE CASES.**

{ No. 5, 9½ x 4¾, in.,  .  .

**ENVELOPE CASES.**

{ No. 2, 8 x 6, in.,  .  .  .

**ENVELOPE CASES.**

{ No. 1, 13½ x 9½, in.,  .

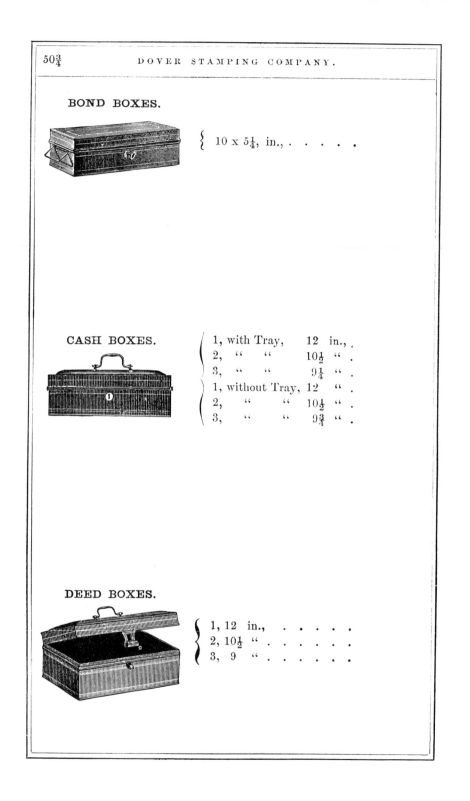

**BOND BOXES.**

$\{$   10 x $5\frac{1}{4}$, in., . . . . .

**CASH BOXES.**

$\{$
1, with Tray,   12   in., .
2,   "   "   $10\frac{1}{2}$   "   .
3,   "   "   $9\frac{1}{4}$   "   .
1, without Tray, 12   "   .
2,   "   "   $10\frac{1}{2}$   "   .
3,   "   "   $9\frac{3}{4}$   "   .

**DEED BOXES.**

$\{$
1, 12   in.,   . . . . .
2, $10\frac{1}{2}$   "   . . . . .
3, 9   "   . . . . .

## CARD RACKS.

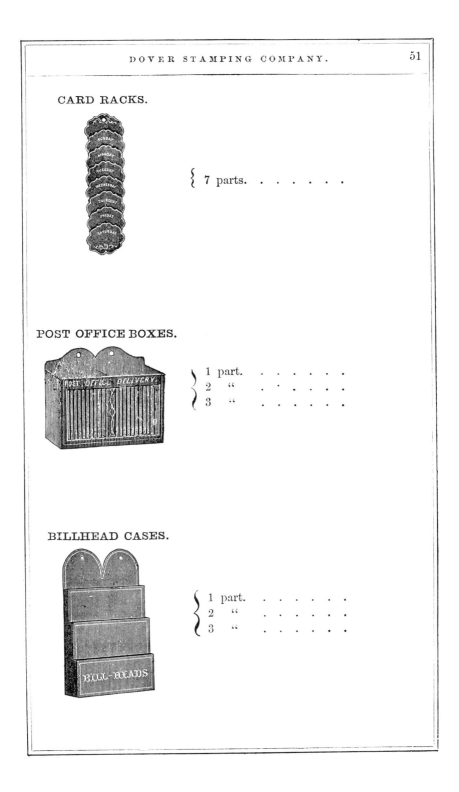

$\{$ 7 parts. . . . . . .

## POST OFFICE BOXES.

$\}$ 1 part. . . . . . .
2 " . . . . . .
3 " . . . . . .

## BILLHEAD CASES.

$\}$ 1 part. . . . . . .
2 " . . . . . .
3 " . . . . . .

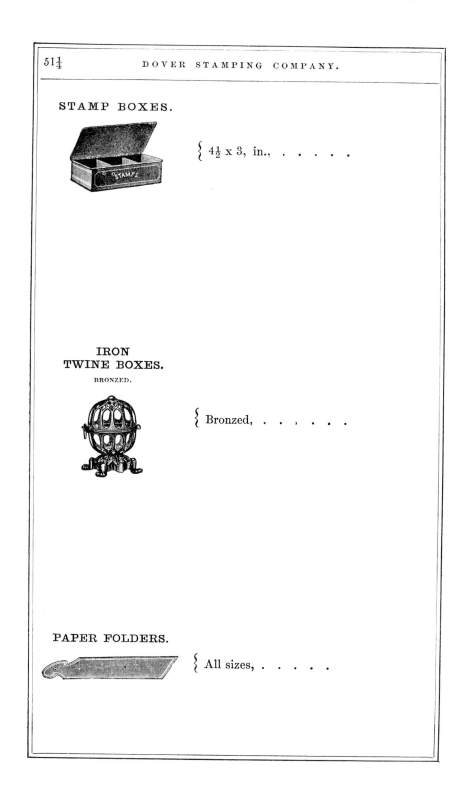

## STAMP BOXES.

$\{$ $4\frac{1}{2}$ x 3, in., . . . . .

## IRON
## TWINE BOXES.
### BRONZED.

$\{$ Bronzed, . . , . . . .

## PAPER FOLDERS.

$\{$ All sizes, . . . . .

| | | |
|---|---|---|
| **BANK NOTICE BOXES.** | 1, 6½ x 3 in., . . . . | |
| | 2, 5 x 2½ " . . . . | |

| | |
|---|---|
| **NEWSPAPER BOXES.** | No. 1, . . . . . . . |
| | " 2, . . . . . . . |

| | |
|---|---|
| **SAND BOXES.** | Bronzed, . . . . . . |
| | Octagon, . . . . . . |

| | |
|---|---|
| **MARKING POTS.** | No. 1, . . . . . . . |

| | |
|---|---|
| **JAPANNED TIN FOR SIGNS.** | 10 x 14 in., . . . . . |
| | 12 x 17 " . . . . . |
| | 14 x 20 " . . . . . |

| | |
|---|---|
| **CALENDERS FOR STEAMERS.** | One Size, . . . . . . |

| | |
|---|---|
| **SCHOLAR'S COMPANION.** | One Size. . . . . . . |

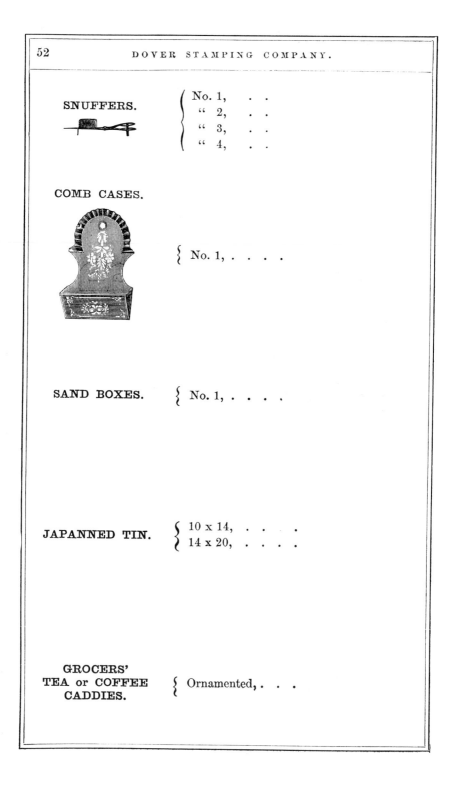

SNUFFERS.

No. 1, . .
" 2, . .
" 3, . .
" 4, . .

COMB CASES.

No. 1, . . . .

SAND BOXES.

No. 1, . . . .

JAPANNED TIN.

10 x 14, . . . .
14 x 20, . . . .

GROCERS'
TEA or COFFEE
CADDIES.

Ornamented, . . .

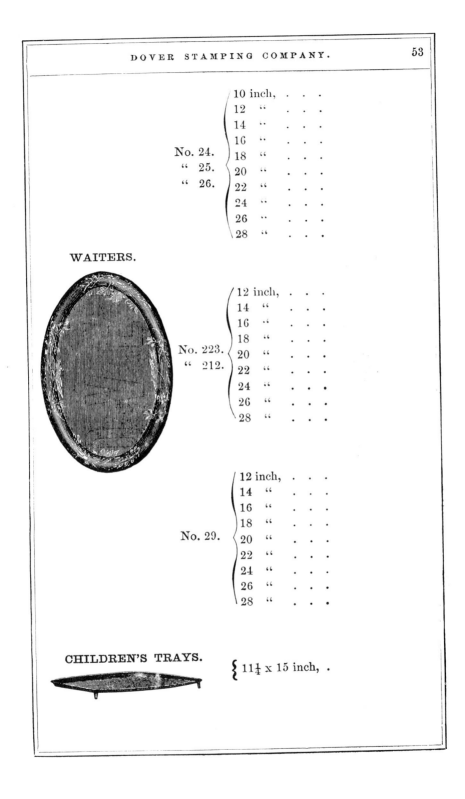

No. 24.
" 25.
" 26.

10 inch, . . .
12 " . . .
14 " . . .
16 " . . .
18 " . . .
20 " . . .
22 " . . .
24 " . . .
26 " . . .
28 " . . .

**WAITERS.**

No. 223.
" 212.

12 inch, . . .
14 " . . .
16 " . . .
18 " . . .
20 " . . .
22 " . . .
24 " . . .
26 " . . .
28 " . . .

No. 29.

12 inch, . . .
14 " . . .
16 " . . .
18 " . . .
20 " . . .
22 " . . .
24 " . . .
26 " . . .
28 " . . .

**CHILDREN'S TRAYS.**

$11\frac{1}{4}$ x 15 inch, .

## JAPANNED
## TIN TOYS.

### STRAIGHT CUPS.

No. 1, . . . .
" 2, . . . .
" 3, . . . .

### FLARING CUPS.

No. 1, . . . .
" 2, . . . .
" 3, · . . .

### HOUSE BANKS.

No. 1, . . . .
" 2, . . . .
Extra Large, .

### GOTHIC BANKS.

No. 1, . . . .
" 2, . . . .

### TRUNKS.

No. 1, . . . .
" 2, . . . .

### COVERED PAILS.

No. 1, . . . .
" 2, . . . .
FANCY. NESTS OF 3.
Pint, Quart, 2 Quart,

JAPANNED
TIN TOYS.

CHAMBER PAILS. { No. 1, . . .

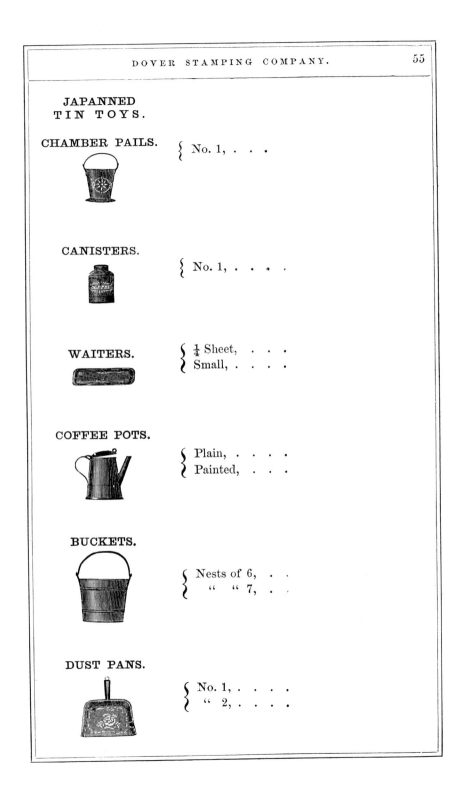

CANISTERS. { No. 1, . . . .

WAITERS. { ¼ Sheet, . . .
{ Small, . . . .

COFFEE POTS. { Plain, . . . .
{ Painted, . . .

BUCKETS. { Nests of 6, . .
{ " " 7, . .

DUST PANS. { No. 1, . . . .
{ " 2, . . . .

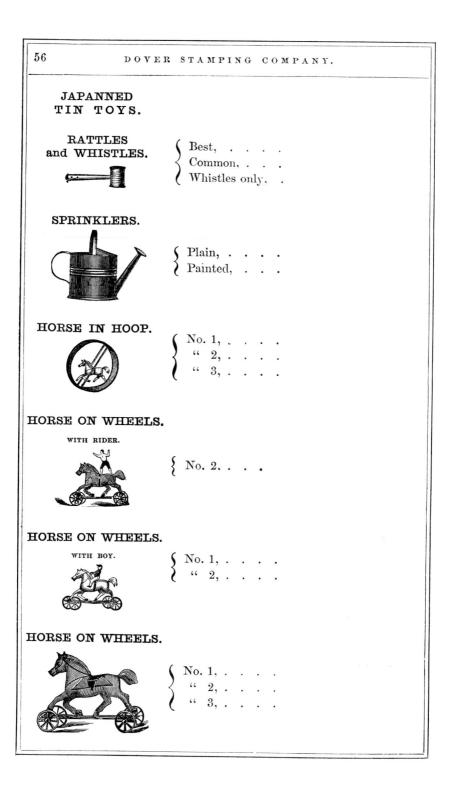

## JAPANNED
## TIN TOYS.

### RATTLES
### and WHISTLES.

Best, . . . .
Common, . . .
Whistles only, . .

### SPRINKLERS.

Plain, . . . .
Painted, . . .

### HORSE IN HOOP.

No. 1, . . . .
" 2, . . . .
" 3, . . . .

### HORSE ON WHEELS.

#### WITH RIDER.

No. 2. . . .

### HORSE ON WHEELS.

#### WITH BOY.

No. 1, . . . .
" 2, . . . .

### HORSE ON WHEELS.

No. 1, . . . .
" 2, . . . .
" 3, . . . .

## JAPANNED
## TIN TOYS.

### GIGS.

{ With No. 2 horse, . .
  "   " 3 "   . .

### WATER TROWS.

{ With No. 3 horse, . .

### DUMP CARTS.

No. 1, with No. 1 horse,
  " 2,  "  " 2 "
  " 3,  ..  " 3 "

### EXPRESS WAGONS.

No. 1, . . . . . .
  " 2, . . . . . .
  " 3, . . . . . .
  " 4, . . . . . .

### EXPRESS WAGONS.
WITH HORSES.

No. 1, 2 No. 1 horses,
  " 2, 2 " 2 "
  " 3, 1 " 1 "
  " 4, 1 " 2 "

### BUGGIES.

1 No. 1 Horse & Driver,
1 " 2 " " "
2 " 3 " " "
1 " 1 " no "
2 " 2 " " "

### ASSORTED ANIMALS.

{ Lion, Tiger, Leopard,
Cow, Horse, Elephant,
In one package, . .

## JAPANNED TIN TOYS.

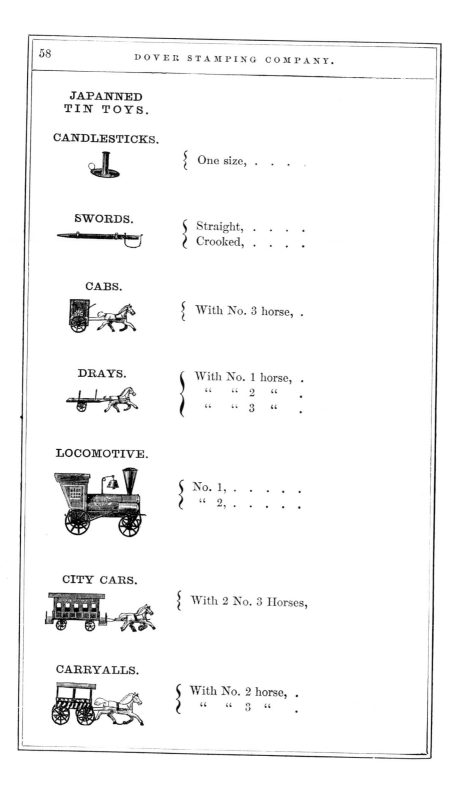

### CANDLESTICKS.

One size, . . . .

### SWORDS.

Straight, . . . .
Crooked, . . . .

### CABS.

With No. 3 horse, .

### DRAYS.

With No. 1 horse, .
" " 2 " .
" " 3 " .

### LOCOMOTIVE.

No. 1, . . . . .
" 2, . . . . .

### CITY CARS.

With 2 No. 3 Horses,

### CARRYALLS.

With No. 2 horse, .
" " 3 " .

## CAST IRON TOYS.

### FRUIT BASKETS.

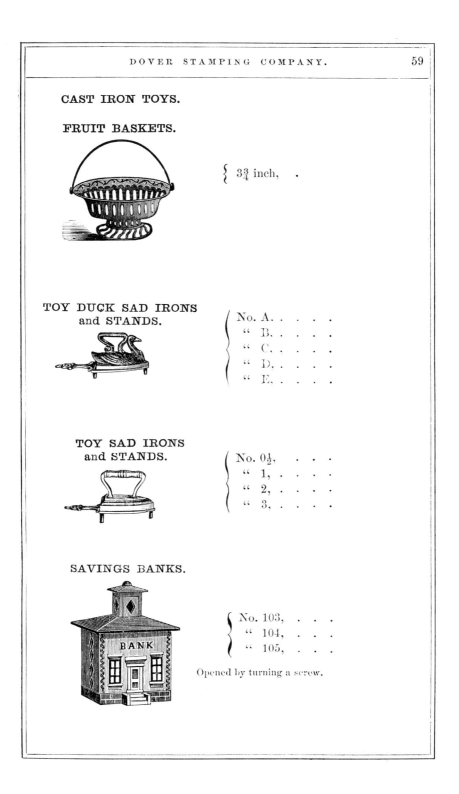

{ 3¾ inch, .

### TOY DUCK SAD IRONS and STANDS.

{ No. A . . . . .
  " B. . . . .
  " C. . . . .
  " D. . . . .
  " E. . . . .

### TOY SAD IRONS and STANDS.

{ No. 0½, . . .
  " 1, . . . .
  " 2, . . . .
  " 3, . . . .

### SAVINGS BANKS.

BANK

{ No. 103, . . .
  " 104, . . .
  " 105, . . .

Opened by turning a screw.

## WATER COOLERS.

$1\frac{1}{2}$ gallons, . . . . .

2 " . . . . .

3 " . . . . .

4 " . . . . .

6 " . . . . .

10 " . . . . .

Various Colors and Ornaments.

*Howland Hse.*

## CHAMBER, or SLOP PAILS.

| | Diameter. Breast. | |
|---|---|---|
| No. 100, | $12\frac{1}{4}$ inch, | Green, |
| " 200, | $11\frac{1}{4}$ " | " |
| " 250, | $11\frac{1}{4}$ " | " |
| " 350, | 10 " | " |
| " 100, | Oak or Paneled, | |
| " 200, | " " | " |
| " 250, | " " | " |
| " 350, | " " | " |
| " 100, | Oak, with Band, | |
| " 200, | " " | " |
| " 250, | " " | " |
| " 350, | " " | " |

Nos. 100, 200 are of **IX** tin; 250, 350 are of **IC** tin.

## WATER SPRINKLERS.

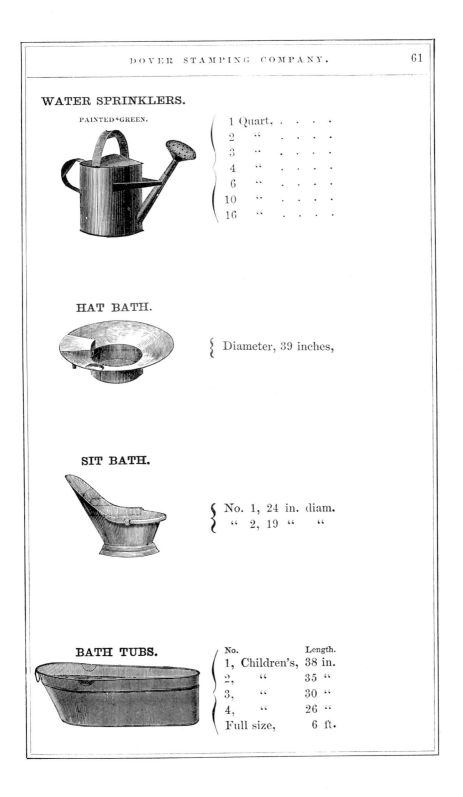

PAINTED GREEN.

1 Quart, . . . .
2 " . . . .
3 " . . . .
4 " . . . .
6 " . . . .
10 " . . . .
16 " . . . .

## HAT BATH.

Diameter, 39 inches,

## SIT BATH.

No. 1, 24 in. diam.
" 2, 19 "    "

## BATH TUBS.

| No. | | Length. |
|---|---|---|
| 1, | Children's, | 38 in. |
| 2, | " | 35 " |
| 3, | " | 30 " |
| 4, | " | 26 " |
| Full size, | | 6 ft. |

## TOILET WARE.

## BOSTON PATTERN.

IN RED, GREEN AND BLUE.

Toilet Ware, with Round Covered Carriers, — as in Boston Pattern,

finished in Oak, Plain,   . . . . . . . .   .
"       " Oak, Gilt Band, . . . . . . .   .
"       " Black Walnut, Plain,   . . . . . .
"       " Black Walnut, Gilt Band, . . . . . .
"       " Light Colors, Paneled, . . . . . .
"       " Landscape, . . . . . . . .   .
"       " Novelty Stripe, . . . . . . .   .
"       " Autumn Leaf,   . . . . . . .   .
"       " Rustic, with Flowers or Leaf,   . . .
"       " Rustic, Plain, . . . . . . . .   .
"       " Light or Black Ground, Ornamented, .
"       " Panel, with Flowers,   . . . . . .
"       " Light Colors or Green, Plain,   . . .

# TOILET WARE.

## DOVER PATTERN.

RICHLY ORNAMENTED.

RED, BLUE, GREEN.

## SERPENTINE PATTERN.

RICHLY ORNAMENTED.

RED, BLUE, GREEN.

## LIP PAIL CARRIER.

Finished in Oak, Plain, . . . . . . . . .
  "  " Oak, Gilt Band, . . . . . . .
  "  " Black Walnut, Plain, . . . . .
  "  " Black Walnut, Gilt Band, . . . .
  "  " Light Colors or Green, Plain, . .
  "  " Light Colors, Paneled, . . . . .
  "  " Light Colors, Paneled with Flowers,
  "  " Light Colors, Gilt Band, . . . .
  "  " Light Colors, Ornamented, . . .
  "  " White, Carmine Band, . . . . .

## OVAL CARRIER.

Finished in Oak, Plain, . . . . . . . . .
  "  " Oak, Gilt Band, . . . . . . .
  "  " Black Walnut, Plain, . . . . .
  "  " Black Walnut, Gilt Band, . . . .
  "  " Light Colors or Green, Plain, . .
  "  " Light Colors, Paneled, . . . . .
  "  " Light Colors, Paneled with Flowers,
  "  " Light Colors, Gilt Band, . . . .
  "  " Light Colors, Ornamented. . . .
  "  " Autumn Leaf, . . . . . . . .
  "  " Rustic, with Flowers with Leaf, . .
  "  " Rustic, Plain, . . . . . . . .

## TOILET WARE.

### WATER CARRIERS.

**HIGH COVERED CARRIERS.**
- Extra Finish, . . . . . . .
- Gold Band, . . . . . . .
- Paneled, . . . . . . . .
- Plain, . . . . . . . . .
- Oak or Black Walnut, Plain, .
- Oak or Black Walnut, Gilt Band,

**OVAL CARRIERS.**
- Extra Finish, . . . . . . .
- Gold Band, . . . . . . .
- Paneled, . . . . . . . .
- Plain, . . . . . . . . .
- Oak or Black Walnut, Plain, .
- Oak or Black Walnut, Gilt Band,

**TOILET JARS.**
- Extra Finish, . . . . . . .
- Gold Band, . . . . . . .
- Paneled, . . . . . . . .
- Plain, . . . . . . . . .
- Oak or Black Walnut, Plain, .
- Oak or Black Walnut, Gilt Band,

**FOOT TUBS.**
- Extra Finish, . . . . . . .
- Gold Band, . . . . . . .
- Paneled, . . . . . . . .
- Plain, . . . . . . . . .
- Oak or Black Walnut, Plain, .
- Oak or Black Walnut, Gilt Band,

## TOILET WARE.

## LIP PAILS.

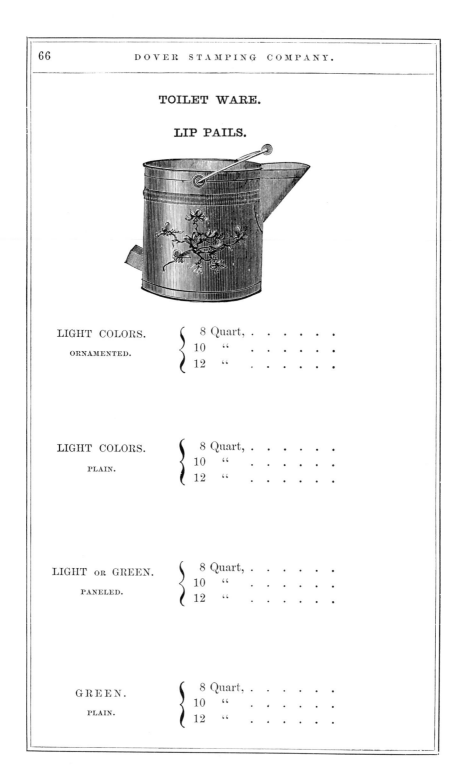

**LIGHT COLORS.**
ORNAMENTED.
{ 8 Quart, . . . . . .
10 " . . . . . .
12 " . . . . . .

**LIGHT COLORS.**
PLAIN.
{ 8 Quart, . . . . . .
10 " . . . . . .
12 " . . . . . .

**LIGHT or GREEN.**
PANELED.
{ 8 Quart, . . . . . .
10 " . . . . . .
12 " . . . . . .

**GREEN.**
PLAIN.
{ 8 Quart, . . . . . .
10 " . . . . . .
12 " . . . . . .

# FRENCH TINNED IRON GOODS.

We call particular attention to

## OUR MANUFACTURES

OF

## TINNED IRON WARES,

### THEIR QUALITY AND FINISH,

and assure our Patrons that we shall faithfully adhere to the

## HIGH STANDARD

established by us, in the production of this

## NEW LINE OF GOODS.

The appreciation already accorded our efforts by the Trade—
and the encouragement offered us—warrants a constant increase
in variety—and the almost daily offering of NEW ARTICLES.

# FRENCH
# TINNED IRON WARE.

## DEEP CAKE PANS.
### TINNED.

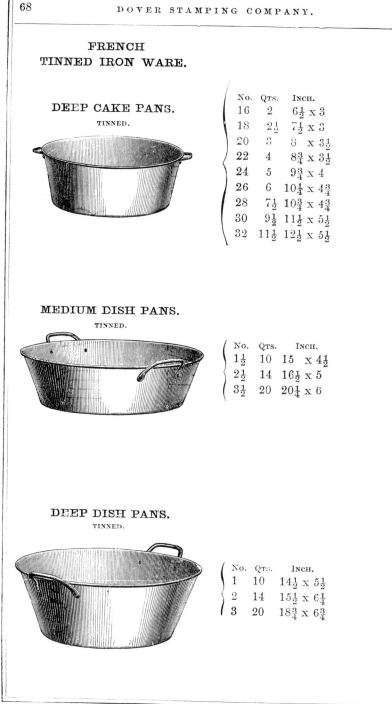

| No. | QTS. | INCH. |
|-----|------|-------|
| 16 | 2 | $6\frac{1}{2}$ x 3 |
| 18 | $2\frac{1}{2}$ | $7\frac{1}{2}$ x 3 |
| 20 | 3 | 8 x $3\frac{1}{2}$ |
| 22 | 4 | $8\frac{3}{4}$ x $3\frac{1}{2}$ |
| 24 | 5 | $9\frac{3}{4}$ x 4 |
| 26 | 6 | $10\frac{1}{4}$ x $4\frac{3}{4}$ |
| 28 | $7\frac{1}{2}$ | $10\frac{3}{4}$ x $4\frac{3}{4}$ |
| 30 | $9\frac{1}{2}$ | $11\frac{1}{2}$ x $5\frac{1}{2}$ |
| 32 | $11\frac{1}{2}$ | $12\frac{1}{2}$ x $5\frac{1}{2}$ |

## MEDIUM DISH PANS.
### TINNED.

| No. | QTS. | INCH. |
|-----|------|-------|
| $1\frac{1}{2}$ | 10 | 15 x $4\frac{1}{2}$ |
| $2\frac{1}{2}$ | 14 | $16\frac{1}{2}$ x 5 |
| $3\frac{1}{2}$ | 20 | $20\frac{1}{4}$ x 6 |

## DEEP DISH PANS.
### TINNED.

| No. | QTS. | INCH. |
|-----|------|-------|
| 1 | 10 | $14\frac{1}{2}$ x $5\frac{1}{2}$ |
| 2 | 14 | $15\frac{1}{2}$ x $6\frac{1}{4}$ |
| 3 | 20 | $18\frac{3}{4}$ x $6\frac{3}{4}$ |

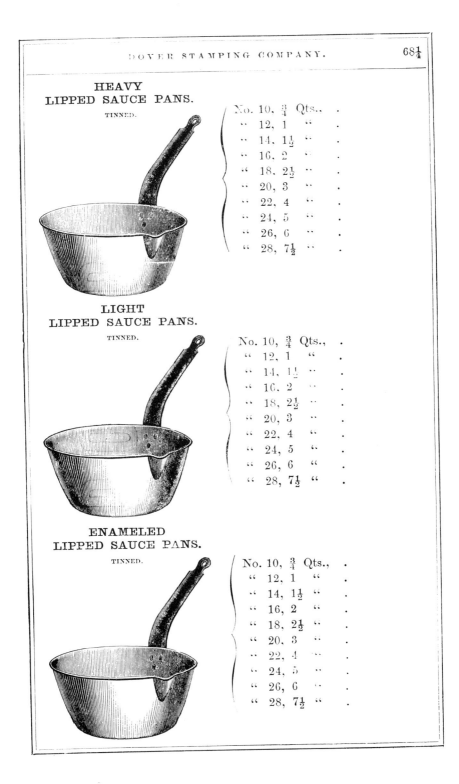

### HEAVY
### LIPPED SAUCE PANS.

TINNED.

| | | |
|---|---|---|
| No. 10, | ¾ Qts.. | . |
| " 12, | 1 " | . |
| " 14, | 1½ " | . |
| " 16, | 2 " | . |
| " 18, | 2½ " | . |
| " 20, | 3 " | . |
| " 22, | 4 " | . |
| " 24, | 5 " | . |
| " 26, | 6 " | . |
| " 28, | 7½ " | . |

### LIGHT
### LIPPED SAUCE PANS.

TINNED.

| | | |
|---|---|---|
| No. 10, | ¾ Qts., | . |
| " 12, | 1 " | . |
| " 14, | 1½ " | . |
| " 16, | 2 " | . |
| " 18, | 2½ " | . |
| " 20, | 3 " | . |
| " 22, | 4 " | . |
| " 24, | 5 " | . |
| " 26, | 6 " | . |
| " 28, | 7½ " | . |

### ENAMELED
### LIPPED SAUCE PANS.

TINNED.

| | | |
|---|---|---|
| No. 10, | ¾ Qts., | . |
| " 12, | 1 " | . |
| " 14, | 1½ " | . |
| " 16, | 2 " | . |
| " 18, | 2½ " | . |
| " 20, | 3 " | . |
| " 22, | 4 " | . |
| " 24, | 5 " | . |
| " 26, | 6 " | . |
| " 28, | 7½ " | . |

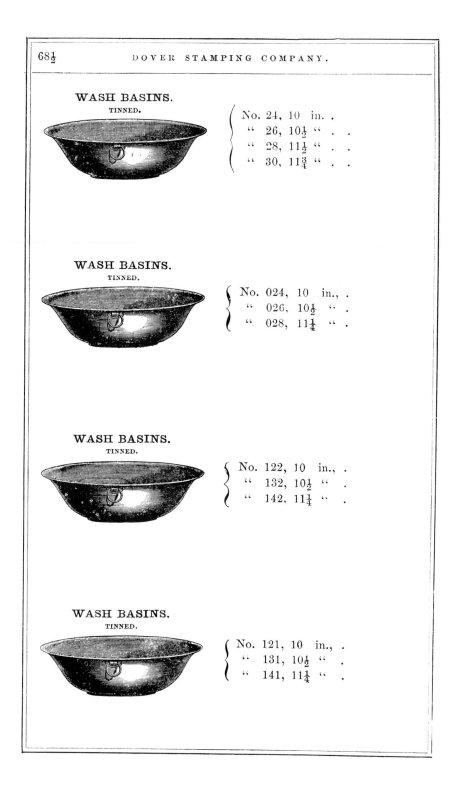

**WASH BASINS.**
TINNED.

No. 24, 10 in. . .
" 26, 10½ " . .
" 28, 11½ " . .
" 30, 11¾ " . .

**WASH BASINS.**
TINNED.

No. 024, 10 in., .
" 026, 10½ " .
" 028, 11¼ " .

**WASH BASINS.**
TINNED.

No. 122, 10 in., .
" 132, 10½ " .
" 142, 11¼ " .

**WASH BASINS.**
TINNED.

No. 121, 10 in., .
" 131, 10½ " .
" 141, 11¼ " .

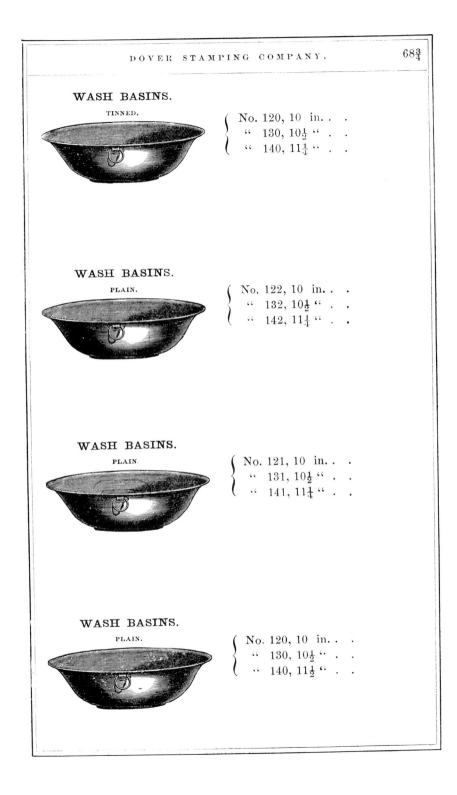

## WASH BASINS.

TINNED.

No. 120, 10 in. . .
"  130, 10½ " . .
"  140, 11¼ " . .

## WASH BASINS.

PLAIN.

No. 122, 10 in. . .
"  132, 10½ " . .
"  142, 11¼ " . .

## WASH BASINS.

PLAIN.

No. 121, 10 in. . .
"  131, 10½ " . .
"  141, 11¼ " . .

## WASH BASINS.

PLAIN.

No. 120, 10 in. . .
"  130, 10½ " . .
"  140, 11½ " . .

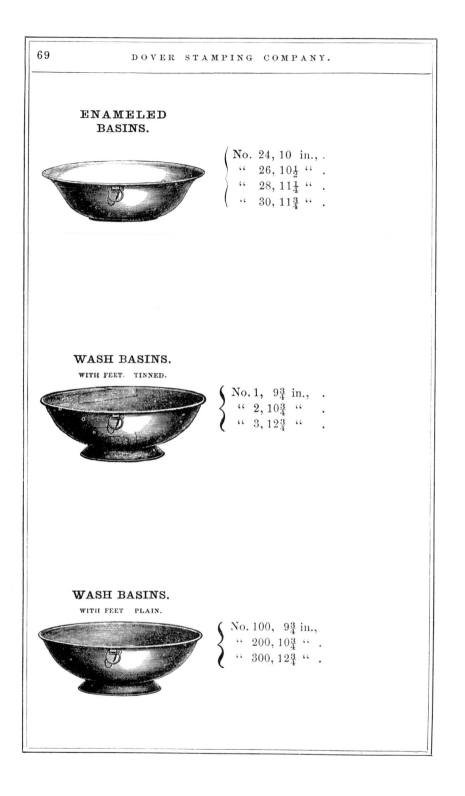

### ENAMELED BASINS.

$\left\{\begin{array}{l}\end{array}\right.$ No. 24, 10 in., .
    "  26, 10½ " .
    "  28, 11¼ " .
    "  30, 11¾ " .

### WASH BASINS.

WITH FEET. TINNED.

No. 1,  9¾ in.,  .
 " 2, 10¾ "   .
 " 3, 12¾ "   .

### WASH BASINS.

WITH FEET  PLAIN.

No. 100,  9¾ in.,
 " 200, 10¾ "  .
 " 300, 12¾ "  .

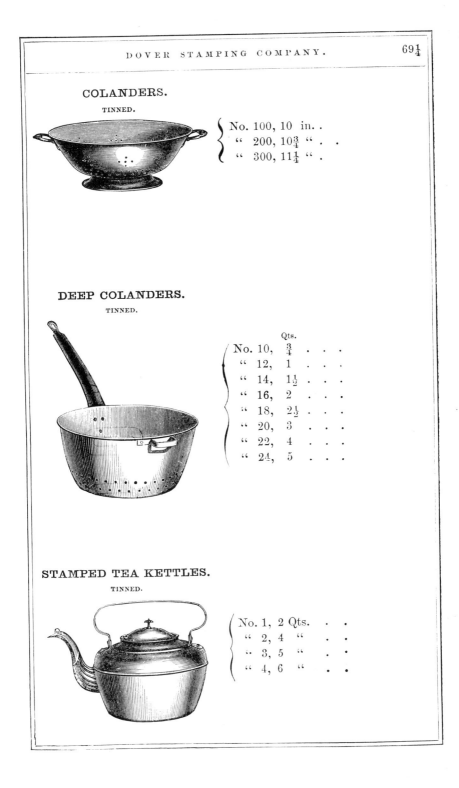

## COLANDERS.

TINNED.

> No. 100, 10 in . .
> " 200, 10¾ " . .
> " 300, 11¼ " .

## DEEP COLANDERS.

TINNED.

|  | Qts. |  |  |  |
|---|---|---|---|---|
| No. 10, | ¾ | . | . | . |
| " 12, | 1 | . | . | . |
| " 14, | 1½ | . | . | . |
| " 16, | 2 | . | . | . |
| " 18, | 2½ | . | . | . |
| " 20, | 3 | . | . | . |
| " 22, | 4 | . | . | . |
| " 24, | 5 | . | . | . |

## STAMPED TEA KETTLES.

TINNED.

> No. 1, 2 Qts. . .
> " 2, 4 " . .
> " 3, 5 " . .
> " 4, 6 " . .

**FLARING MILK PANS.**

TINNED.

| | |
|---|---|
| ½ | Pint, . . . . . |
| 1 | " . . . . |
| 2 | " . . . . |
| 3 | " . . . . |
| 2 | Qts., . . . . |
| 3 | " . . . . |
| 4 | " . . . . |
| 6 | " . . . . |
| 10 | " 15 in., . . . |
| 10 | " 16 " . . . |

**FLARING MILK PANS.**

PLAIN.

| | |
|---|---|
| ½ | Pint, . . . . . |
| 1 | " . . . . |
| 2 | " . . . . |
| 3 | " . . . . |
| 2 | Qts., . . . . |
| 3 | " . . . . |
| 4 | " . . . . |
| 6 | " . . . . |
| 10 | " 15 in., . . . |
| 10 | " 16 " . . . |

**STRAIGHT MILK PANS.**

TINNED.

| | | |
|---|---|---|
| ½ | Qts., | $4\frac{3}{4}$ x 2, . |
| 1 | " | $6\frac{1}{2}$ x 2, . |
| 1½ | " | $7\frac{1}{4}$ x 2, . |
| 2 | " | 8 x $2\frac{1}{4}$, . |
| 3 | " | $8\frac{3}{4}$ x $2\frac{1}{4}$, . |
| 3½ | " | $9\frac{5}{8}$ x $2\frac{1}{2}$, . |
| 4 | " | $10\frac{1}{2}$ x $2\frac{5}{8}$, . |
| 6 | " | $12\frac{1}{4}$ x $2\frac{3}{4}$, . |
| 10 | " | 15 x 3, . |

**STRAIGHT MILK PANS.**

PLAIN.

| | | |
|---|---|---|
| ½ | Qts., | $4\frac{3}{4}$ x 2. . |
| 1 | " | $6\frac{1}{2}$ x 2, . |
| 1½ | " | $7\frac{1}{4}$ x 2, . |
| 2 | " | 8 x $2\frac{1}{4}$, . |
| 3 | " | $8\frac{3}{4}$ x $2\frac{1}{4}$, . |
| 3½ | " | $9\frac{5}{8}$ x $2\frac{1}{2}$, . |
| 4 | " | $10\frac{1}{2}$ x $2\frac{5}{8}$, . |
| 6 | " | $12\frac{1}{4}$ x $2\frac{3}{4}$, . |
| 10 | " | 15 x 3, . |

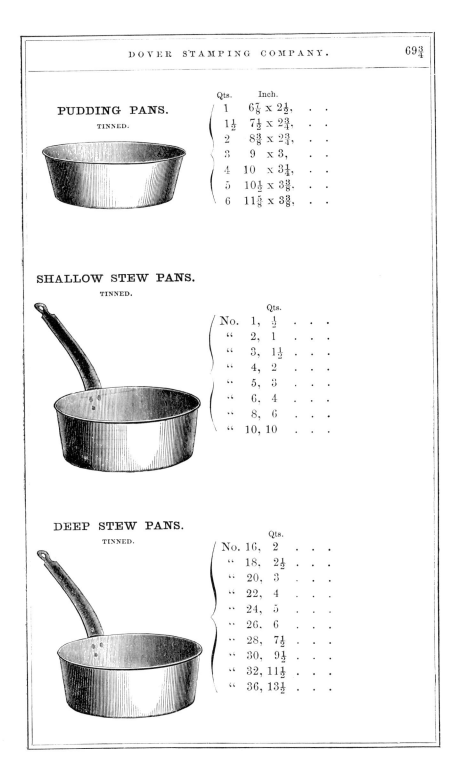

## PUDDING PANS.
### TINNED.

| Qts. | Inch. | | |
|---|---|---|---|
| 1 | $6\frac{7}{8}$ x $2\frac{1}{2}$, | . | . |
| $1\frac{1}{2}$ | $7\frac{1}{2}$ x $2\frac{3}{4}$, | . | . |
| 2 | $8\frac{3}{8}$ x $2\frac{3}{4}$, | . | . |
| 3 | 9 x 3, | . | . |
| 4 | 10 x $3\frac{1}{4}$, | . | . |
| 5 | $10\frac{1}{2}$ x $3\frac{3}{8}$. | . | . |
| 6 | $11\frac{5}{8}$ x $3\frac{3}{8}$, | . | . |

## SHALLOW STEW PANS.
### TINNED.

| | | Qts. | | |
|---|---|---|---|---|
| No. | 1, | $\frac{1}{2}$ | . . | . |
| " | 2, | 1 | . . | . |
| " | 3, | $1\frac{1}{2}$ | . . | . |
| " | 4, | 2 | . . | . |
| " | 5, | 3 | . . | . |
| " | 6, | 4 | . . | . |
| " | 8, | 6 | . . | . |
| " | 10, | 10 | . . | . |

## DEEP STEW PANS.
### TINNED.

| | | Qts. | | |
|---|---|---|---|---|
| No. | 16, | 2 | . . | . |
| " | 18, | $2\frac{1}{2}$ | . . | . |
| " | 20, | 3 | . . | . |
| " | 22, | 4 | . . | . |
| " | 24, | 5 | . . | . |
| " | 26. | 6 | . . | . |
| " | 28, | $7\frac{1}{2}$ | . . | . |
| " | 30, | $9\frac{1}{2}$ | . . | . |
| " | 32, | $11\frac{1}{2}$ | . . | . |
| " | 36, | $13\frac{1}{2}$ | . . | . |

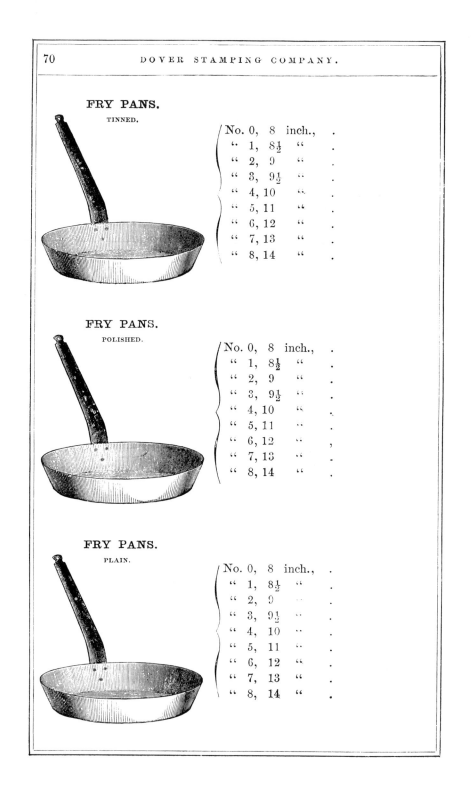

## FRY PANS.

TINNED.

No. 0,  8  inch.,  .
"  1,  8½  "  .
"  2,  9  "  .
"  3,  9½  "  .
"  4, 10  "  .
"  5, 11  "  .
"  6, 12  "  .
"  7, 13  "  .
"  8, 14  "  .

## FRY PANS.

POLISHED.

No. 0,  8  inch.,  .
"  1,  8½  "  .
"  2,  9  "  .
"  3,  9½  "  .
"  4, 10  "  .
"  5, 11  "  .
"  6, 12  "  ,
"  7, 13  "  .
"  8, 14  "  .

## FRY PANS.

PLAIN.

No. 0,  8  inch.,  .
"  1,  8½  "  .
"  2,  9  "  .
"  3,  9½  "  .
"  4, 10  "  .
"  5, 11  "  .
"  6, 12  "  .
"  7, 13  "  .
"  8, 14  "  .

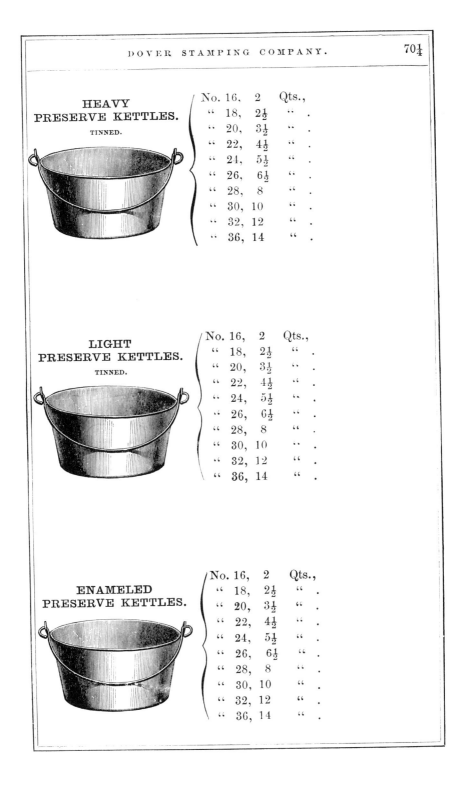

**HEAVY PRESERVE KETTLES.**

TINNED.

No. 16,   2   Qts.,
"   18,   2½   "   .
"   20,   3½   "   .
"   22,   4½   "   .
"   24,   5½   "   .
"   26,   6½   "   .
"   28,   8   "   .
"   30,   10   "   .
"   32,   12   "   .
"   36,   14   "   .

**LIGHT PRESERVE KETTLES.**

TINNED.

No. 16,   2   Qts.,
"   18,   2½   "   .
"   20,   3½   "   .
"   22,   4½   "   .
"   24,   5½   "   .
"   26,   6½   "   .
"   28,   8   "   .
"   30,   10   "   .
"   32,   12   "   .
"   36,   14   "   .

**ENAMELED PRESERVE KETTLES.**

No. 16,   2   Qts.,
"   18,   2½   "   .
"   20,   3½   "   .
"   22,   4½   "   .
"   24,   5½   "   .
"   26,   6½   "   .
"   28,   8   "   .
"   30,   10   "   .
"   32,   12   "   .
"   36,   14   "   .

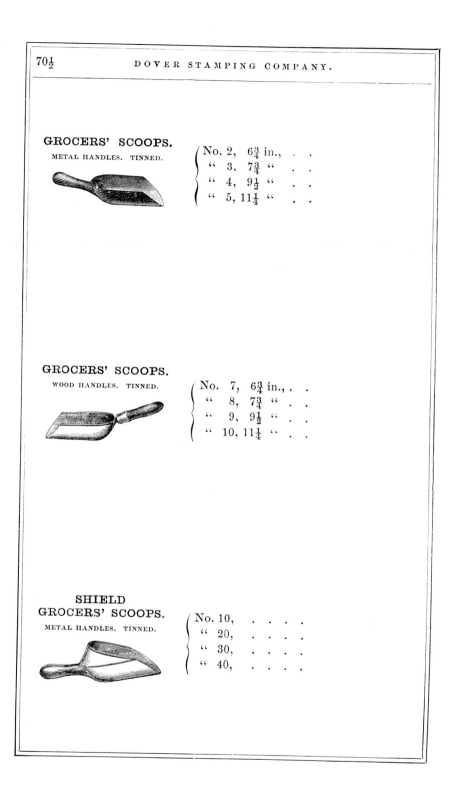

### GROCERS' SCOOPS.

METAL HANDLES. TINNED.

No. 2, 6¾ in., . .
" 3, 7¾ " . .
" 4, 9½ " . .
" 5, 11¼ " . .

### GROCERS' SCOOPS.

WOOD HANDLES. TINNED.

No. 7, 6¾ in., . .
" 8, 7¾ " . .
" 9, 9½ " . .
" 10, 11¼ " . .

### SHIELD
### GROCERS' SCOOPS.

METAL HANDLES. TINNED.

No. 10, . . . .
" 20, . . . .
" 30, . . . .
" 40, . . . .

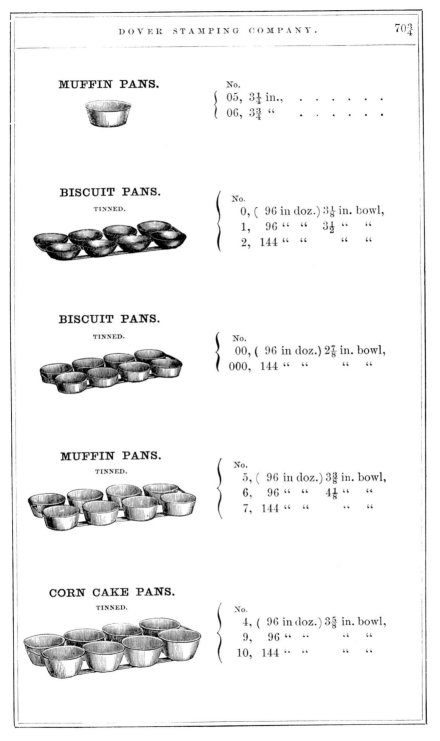

**MUFFIN PANS.**

No.
{ 05, 3$\frac{1}{4}$ in., . . . . . . .
{ 06, 3$\frac{3}{4}$ " . . . . . .

**BISCUIT PANS.**

TINNED.

No.
0, ( 96 in doz.) 3$\frac{1}{8}$ in. bowl,
1, 96 " " 3$\frac{1}{2}$ " "
2, 144 " " " "

**BISCUIT PANS.**

TINNED.

No.
00, ( 96 in doz.) 2$\frac{7}{8}$ in. bowl,
000, 144 " " " "

**MUFFIN PANS.**

TINNED.

No.
5, ( 96 in doz.) 3$\frac{3}{8}$ in. bowl,
6, 96 " " 4$\frac{1}{8}$ " "
7, 144 " " " "

**CORN CAKE PANS.**

TINNED.

No.
4, ( 96 in doz.) 3$\frac{5}{8}$ in. bowl,
9, 96 " " " "
10, 144 " " " "

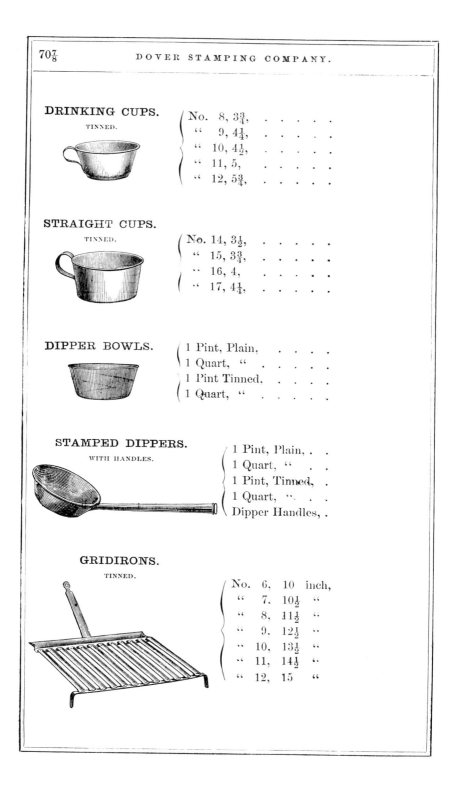

## DRINKING CUPS.

TINNED.

No.  8, 3¾,  . . . . .
"   9, 4¼,  . . . . .
"  10, 4½,  . . . . .
"  11, 5,  . . . . .
"  12, 5¾,  . . . . .

## STRAIGHT CUPS.

TINNED.

No. 14, 3½,  . . . . .
"  15, 3¾,  . . . . .
"  16, 4,  . . . . .
"  17, 4¼,  . . . . .

## DIPPER BOWLS.

1 Pint, Plain,  . . . .
1 Quart, "  . . . . .
1 Pint Tinned,  . . . .
1 Quart, "  . . . . .

## STAMPED DIPPERS.

WITH HANDLES.

1 Pint, Plain, . .
1 Quart, "  . .
1 Pint, Tinned, .
1 Quart, "  . .
Dipper Handles, .

## GRIDIRONS.

TINNED.

No.  6,  10  inch,
"   7,  10½  "
"   8,  11½  "
"   9,  12½  "
"  10,  13½  "
"  11,  14½  "
"  12,  15  "

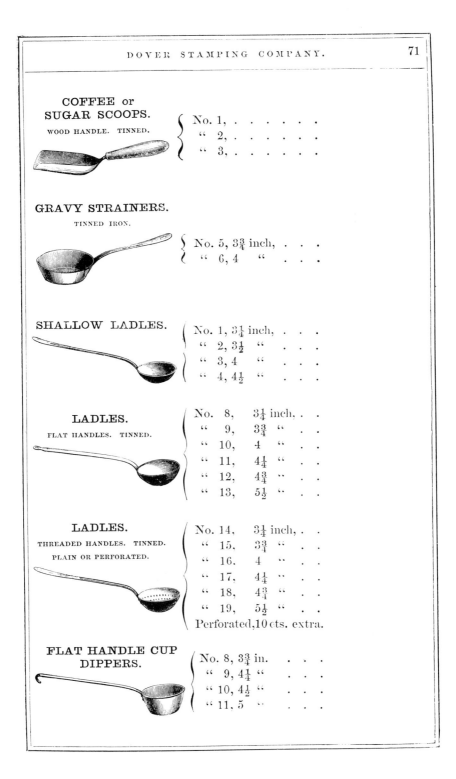

**COFFEE or SUGAR SCOOPS.**

WOOD HANDLE. TINNED.

No. 1, . . . . . .
" 2, . . . . . .
" 3, . . . . . .

**GRAVY STRAINERS.**

TINNED IRON.

No. 5, 3¾ inch, . . .
" 6, 4 " . . .

**SHALLOW LADLES.**

No. 1, 3¼ inch, . . .
" 2, 3½ " . . .
" 3, 4 " . . .
" 4, 4½ " . . .

**LADLES.**

FLAT HANDLES. TINNED.

No. 8, 3¼ inch, . .
" 9, 3¾ " . .
" 10, 4 " . .
" 11, 4¼ " . .
" 12, 4¾ " . .
" 13, 5½ " . .

**LADLES.**

THREADED HANDLES. TINNED.
PLAIN OR PERFORATED.

No. 14, 3¼ inch, . .
" 15, 3¾ " . .
" 16. 4 " . .
" 17, 4¼ " . .
" 18, 4¾ " . .
" 19, 5½ " . .
Perforated, 10 cts. extra.

**FLAT HANDLE CUP DIPPERS.**

No. 8, 3¾ in. . . .
" 9, 4¼ " . . .
" 10, 4½ " . . .
" 11, 5 " . . .

## FRENCH WARE.

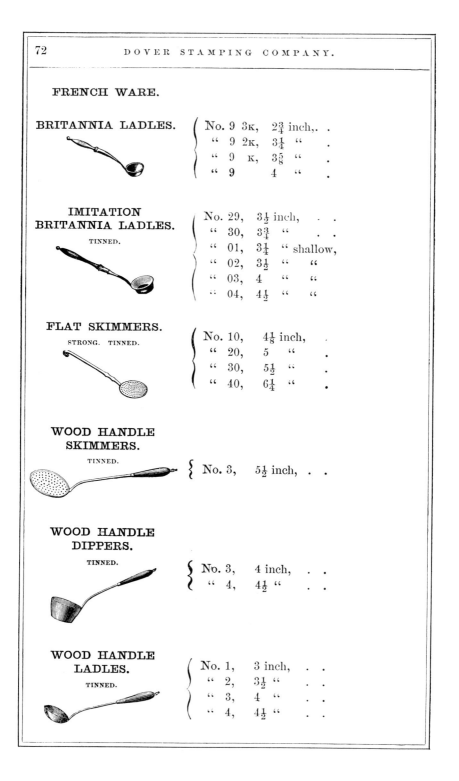

**BRITANNIA LADLES.**

No. 9 3к,   2¾ inch,. .
"   9 2к,   3¼   "    .
"   9   к,   3⅝   "    .
"   9        4    "    .

**IMITATION
BRITANNIA LADLES.**
TINNED.

No. 29,   3½ inch,   . .
"   30,   3¾   "      . .
"   01,   3¼   "  shallow,
"   02,   3½   "    "
"   03,   4    "    "
"   04,   4½   "    "

**FLAT SKIMMERS.**
STRONG.   TINNED.

No. 10,   4⅛ inch,   .
"   20,   5    "      .
"   30,   5½   "      .
"   40,   6¼   "      .

**WOOD HANDLE
SKIMMERS.**
TINNED.

No. 3,   5½ inch,  . .

**WOOD HANDLE
DIPPERS.**
TINNED.

No. 3,   4 inch,   . .
"   4,   4½   "    . .

**WOOD HANDLE
LADLES.**
TINNED.

No. 1,   3 inch,   . .
"   2,   3½  "     . .
"   3,   4   "     . .
"   4,   4½  "     . .

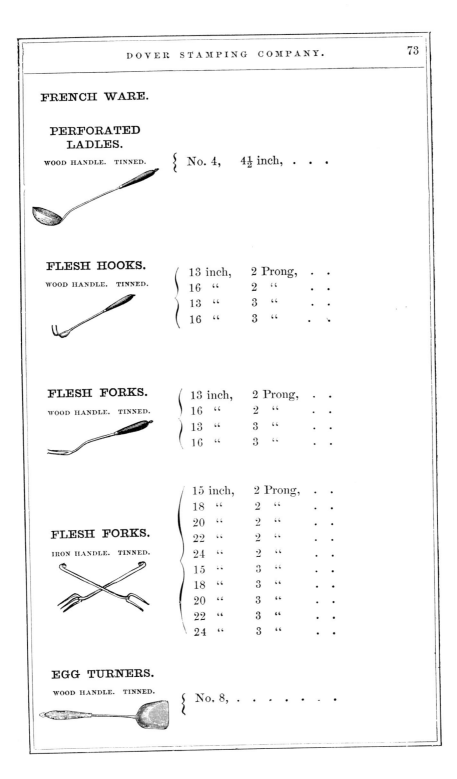

## FRENCH WARE.

### PERFORATED LADLES.
WOOD HANDLE. TINNED.

{ No. 4,    4½ inch, . . .

### FLESH HOOKS.
WOOD HANDLE. TINNED.

{ 13 inch,    2 Prong, . .
 16 "    2 "    . .
 13 "    3 "    . .
 16 "    3 "    . .

### FLESH FORKS.
WOOD HANDLE. TINNED.

{ 13 inch,    2 Prong, . .
 16 "    2 "    . .
 13 "    3 "    . .
 16 "    3 "    . .

### FLESH FORKS.
IRON HANDLE. TINNED.

{ 15 inch,    2 Prong, . .
 18 "    2 "    . .
 20 "    2 "    . .
 22 "    2 "    . .
 24 "    2 "    . .
 15 "    3 "    . .
 18 "    3 "    . .
 20 "    3 "    . .
 22 "    3 "    . .
 24 "    3 "    . .

### EGG TURNERS.
WOOD HANDLE. TINNED.

{ No. 8, . . . . . . .

## CAKE TURNERS.

WOOD HANDLE. TINNED.

{ No. 10, . . . . .

## CAKE TURNERS.

WOOD HANDLE. BRIGHT.

{ No. 1, Russia Iron, .
  " 2,  "   "  .
  " 3, Steel, . . .
  " 4,  "    . . .
  " 5,  "    . . .

## PRESERVE SPOONS.

WOOD HANDLE. TINNED.

{ 10 inch, . . . .
 12  "    . . . .
 15  "    . . . .

## OYSTER or GRAVY LADLE.

{ Plain, . . . . .
 Perforated, . . . .

## COCOA DIPPERS.

{ One size, . . . . .

### TABLE FORKS.
TINNED.

{ No. 24, Threaded, . . . .
" 6, Forged, . . .
" 12, " . . .

### THREADED TABLE SPOONS.
TINNED.

No. 20, Strong, Solid, .
" 21, " " .
" 22, " " .
" 26, " " .

No. 40, Light, Solid, . .
" 41, " " . .
" 216, " " . .
" 217, " " . .

No. 23, Dessert, . . .

### ROUND HANDLE SPOONS.

{ " 11, Table, . . . .
" 9½, Tea, . . . .

### THREADED TEA SPOONS.
TINNED.

{ No. 310, Light, Solid,
" 305, " "
" 117, " "

### FORGED TABLE SPOONS.
TINNED.

{ No. 4, . . . . . .
" 2, . . . . . .
" 13, . . . . . .
" 14, . . . . . .

### FORGED TEA SPOONS.
TINNED.

{ No. 2, . . . . . . .
" 3, . . . . . .

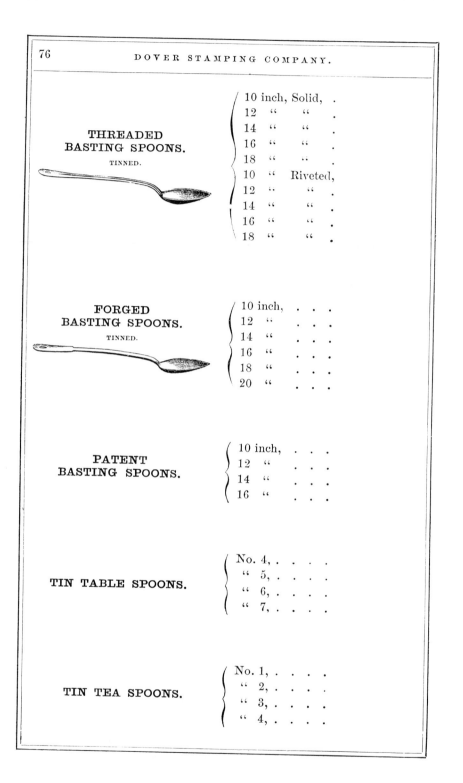

**THREADED
BASTING SPOONS.**
TINNED.

10 inch, Solid, .
12 " " .
14 " " .
16 " " .
18 " " .
10 " Riveted,
12 " " .
14 " " .
16 " " .
18 " " .

**FORGED
BASTING SPOONS.**
TINNED.

10 inch, . . .
12 " . . .
14 " . . .
16 " . . .
18 " . . .
20 " . . .

**PATENT
BASTING SPOONS.**

10 inch, . . .
12 " . . .
14 " . . .
16 " . . .

**TIN TABLE SPOONS.**

No. 4, . . . .
" 5, . . . .
" 6, . . . .
" 7, . . . .

**TIN TEA SPOONS.**

No. 1, . . . .
" 2, . . . .
" 3, . . . .
" 4, . . . .

## BRITANNIA
## TABLE SPOONS.

No.
400, Wire Strengthened,
1390,   "        "
1860,   "        "
1392,   "        "
100,   "        "
1870,   "        "
1862,   "        "
1871,   "        "
1872,   "        "
1874,   "        "
1875,   "        "
1877,   "        "
90,   "        "

## BRITANNIA
## TEA SPOONS.

No.
350, Wire Strengthened,
6900,   "        "
960,   "        "
50,   "        "
970,   "        "
971,   "        "
972,   "        "
974,   "        "
974½,   "        "
6902,   "        "
975.   "        "
977,   "        "
45,   "        "

**SILVER PLATED**
**TABLE SPOONS.**

No.
1880, Argentine, Tipped,
1882,    "        Oval,  .
1886,    "        Olive,  .

**SILVER PLATED**
**TEA SPOONS.**

No.
980, Argentine, Tipped,  .
982,    "        Oval,   .
986,    "        Olive,   .

**SILVER PLATED**
**FORKS.**

Dining,  . . . . .
Medium,  . . . . .
Dessert,  . . . . . .

**SILVER PLATED**
**BUTTER KNIVES.**

Olive,  . . . . . .
Oval,  . . . . . .

**SILVER PLATED**
**FRUIT KNIVES.**

Chased,  . . . . . .

**SILVER PLATED**
**MUSTARD SPOONS.**

Tipped,  . . . . . .
Olive, . . . . . . .

**MASON'S PATENT.**

{ 1 Pint,   . . . . . .

{ 1 Quart,   . . . . . .

{ 2 Quart,   . . . . . .

ABSOLUTE

# PERFECTION,

within the limits of human knowledge, has been attained in this means of

# PRESERVING FRUITS.

It has superseded all other

## GLASS JARS!

In proof of which we need only say that

# THREE THOUSAND GROSS
## (3,000,)

were sold in New England alone in 1867, while more than TEN THOUSAND GROSS were sold during the single year in the country.

With this UNPARALLELED SALE and USE, we challenge any person to name an instance where the articles, if fairly put up, did not KEEP SWEET. It is *simple* beyond comparison, and absolutely certain. It can be opened in a moment without injury to the jar or cover. May be used for years.

Ask your neighbor who has used them, and you will be told there is no trouble in putting up fruit in MASON'S JAR, and that IT KEEPS WHEN PUT UP.

You will also be told by those who are experienced, that all their difficulties heretofore have sprung from experimenting with cheap unphilosophical jars, and that a 9 years test of Mason's, with more than

## EIGHTY THOUSAND GROSS IN USE,

should warrant their adoption by all.

Let your answer to those who importune you to buy new and untried jars, or those not having the indorsement of large experience, be, — "No, sir! I want jars that I know to be

## SIMPLE and CERTAIN."

**WHITNEY'S No. 3 PRESERVE CANS.**

{ 1 Quart, . . . . . .
2 " . . . . . .

Fasten with rosin.

**WILLOUGHBY PAT. PRESERVE CAN.**

SEE CUT, PAGE 15.

{ 1 Quart, . . . . . .
2 "   . . . . . .

This is the most simple, and at the same time most perfect Patent Fastening ever made. Turning a thumb screw closes the can hermetically, or opens it in a moment. It has the unqualified approbation of the public.

**WHITNEY'S No. 1 TIN PRESERVE CANS.**

{ $\frac{2}{3}$ Quart, . . . . . .
1 " . . . . . .
2 " . . . . . .
4 " . . . . . .

These, unlike the generality of Tin Cans in the market, are made for durability — to be used for a term of years. Fastened with rosin, and opened without injury to the cans. Warranted.

**SALVE BOXES.**

{ 1 Ounce, . . . . . .
2 " . . . . . .

## STOVE MICA.

| | Per lb. $ | Per lb. $ | Per lb. $ | Per lb. $ | Per lb. $ |
|---|---|---|---|---|---|
| 2 in. | 2 x 3<br>2 x 3½<br>2 x 4<br>2 x 4½<br>2 x 5 | 2 x 5½<br>2 x 6<br>2 x 6½<br>2 x 7<br>2 x 7½ | 2 x 8<br>2 x 8½<br>.........<br>.........<br>......... | 2 x 9<br>2 x 9½<br>.........<br>.........<br>......... | 2 x 10<br>................<br>................<br>................<br>................ |
| 2½ in. | 2½ x 3<br>2½ x 3½<br>2½ x 4<br>2½ x 4½ | 2½ x 5<br>2½ x 5½<br>2½ x 6<br>2½ x 6½ | 2½ x 7<br>2½ x 7½<br>.........<br>......... | 2½ x 8<br>2½ x 8½<br>2½ x 9<br>2½ x 9½ | 2½ x 10 and upwards.<br>................<br>................<br>................ |
| 3 in. | 3 x 3<br>3 x 3½<br>3 x 4<br>3 x 4½ | 3 x 5<br>3 x 5½<br>.........<br>......... | 3 x 6<br>3 x 6½<br>3 x 7<br>3 x 7½ | 3 x 8<br>3 x 8½<br>3 x 9<br>......... | 3 x 9½<br>................<br>................<br>................ |
| 3½ in. | 3½ x 3½<br>3½ x 4<br>...........<br>........... | 3½ x 4½<br>3½ x 5<br>3½ x 5½<br>.......... | 3½ x 6<br>3½ x 6½<br>3½ x 7<br>3½ x 7½ | 3½ x 8<br>3½ x 8½<br>3½ x 9<br>......... | 3½ x 9½ and upwards.<br>................<br>................<br>................ |
| 4 in. | .........<br>.........<br>.........<br>......... | 4 x 4<br>4 x 4½<br>.........<br>......... | 4 x 5<br>4 x 5½<br>4 x 6<br>4 x 6½ | 4 x 7<br>4 x 7½<br>4 x 8<br>4 x 8½ | 4 x 9<br>................<br>................<br>................ |
| 4½ in. | .........<br>.........<br>.........<br>......... | ..........<br>.........<br>.........<br>......... | 4½ x 4½<br>4½ x 5<br>4½ x 5½<br>4½ x 6<br>.......... | 4½ x 6½<br>4½ x 7<br>4½ x 7½<br>4½ x 8<br>4½ x 8½ | 4½ x 9<br><br><br>................<br>................ |
| 5 in. | .........<br>.........<br>.........<br>......... | ..........<br>.........<br>.........<br>......... | 5 x 5<br>5 x 5½<br>5 x 6<br>5 x 6½ | 5 x 7<br>5 x 7½<br>5 x 8<br>5 x 8½ | 5 x 9<br>................<br>................<br>................ |
| 5½ in. | .........<br>.........<br>.........<br>......... | ..........<br>.........<br>.........<br>......... | 5½ x 5½<br>5½ x 6<br>5½ x 6½<br>.......... | 5½ x 7<br>5½ x 7½<br>5½ x 8<br>5½ x 8½ | 5½ x 9<br>................<br>................<br> |
| 6 in. | .........<br>.........<br>.........<br>......... | ..........<br>.........<br>.........<br>......... | 6 x 6<br>6 x 6½<br>..........<br>.......... | 6 x 7<br>6 x 7½<br>6 x 8<br>6 x 8½ | 6 x 9 and upwards.<br>................<br>................<br>................ |
| 7 in. | .........<br>......... | ..........<br>.......... | ..........<br>.......... | 7 x 7<br>7 x 7½ | 7 x 8 and upwards.<br>................ |
| 8 to 12 in. | .........<br>.........<br>......... | ..........<br>.........<br>......... | ..........<br>.........<br>......... | .........<br>.........<br>......... | 8 x 8 and upwards.<br>9 x 9    "        "<br>10 x 10   "        " |

# TINNERS,

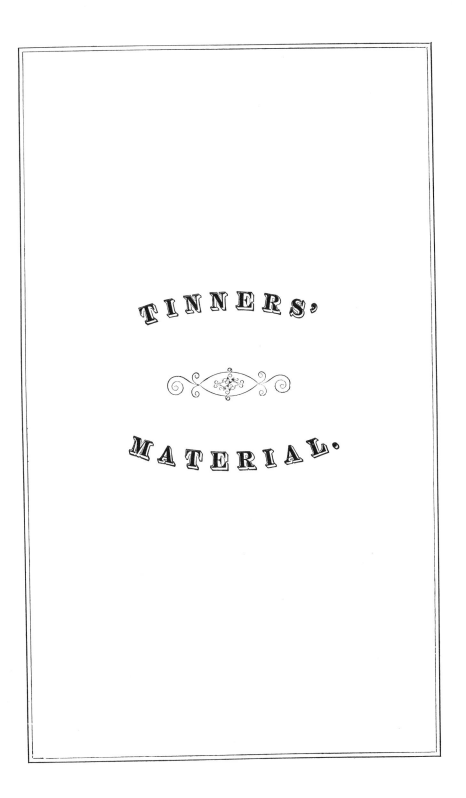

# MATERIAL.

EARS.

FRENCH TINNED
KETTLE EARS.

$\left\{\begin{array}{l}\text{No. 1,} \quad . \quad . \quad . \quad . \\ \text{`` 2,} \quad . \quad . \quad . \quad . \\ \text{`` 3,} \quad . \quad . \quad . \quad . \\ \text{`` 4,} \quad . \quad . \quad . \quad . \\ \text{`` 5,} \quad . \quad . \quad . \quad . \\ \text{`` 6,} \quad . \quad . \quad . \quad . \\ \text{`` 7,} \quad . \quad . \quad . \quad . \end{array}\right.$

FRENCH TINNED
TEA KETTLE EARS.

$\left\{\begin{array}{l}\text{No. 4,} \quad . \quad . \quad . \quad . \\ \text{`` 5,} \quad . \quad . \quad . \quad . \\ \text{`` 6,} \quad . \quad . \quad . \quad . \\ \text{`` 7,} \quad . \quad . \quad . \quad . \end{array}\right.$

TINNED IRON
KETTLE EARS.

$\left\{\begin{array}{l}\text{No. 1,} \quad . \quad . \quad . \quad . \\ \text{`` 2,} \quad . \quad . \quad . \quad . \\ \text{`` 3,} \quad . \quad . \quad . \quad . \\ \text{`` 4,} \quad . \quad . \quad . \quad . \\ \text{`` 5,} \quad . \quad . \quad . \quad . \\ \text{`` 6,} \quad . \quad . \quad . \quad . \\ \text{`` 7,} \quad . \quad . \quad . \quad . \\ \text{`` 8,} \quad . \quad . \quad . \quad . \end{array}\right.$

TINNED IRON
TEA KETTLE EARS.

$\left\{\begin{array}{l}\text{No. 4,} \quad . \quad . \quad . \quad . \\ \text{`` 5,} \quad . \quad . \quad . \quad . \\ \text{`` 6,} \quad . \quad . \quad . \quad . \end{array}\right.$

PRESSED TIN
KETTLE EARS.

$\left\{\begin{array}{l}\text{No. 0,} \quad . \quad . \quad . \quad . \\ \text{`` 1,} \quad . \quad . \quad . \quad . \\ \text{`` 2,} \quad . \quad . \quad . \quad . \\ \text{`` 3,} \quad . \quad . \quad . \quad . \\ \text{`` 4,} \quad . \quad . \quad . \quad . \\ \text{`` 5,} \quad . \quad . \quad . \quad . \\ \text{`` 6,} \quad . \quad . \quad . \quad . \end{array}\right.$

PAINT PAIL EARS.

$\left\{\text{1 inch,} \quad . \quad . \quad . \quad . \right.$

These are of Pressed Tin.  Round.  Receives and hides
the end of the bail in the center.

## RIVETS.

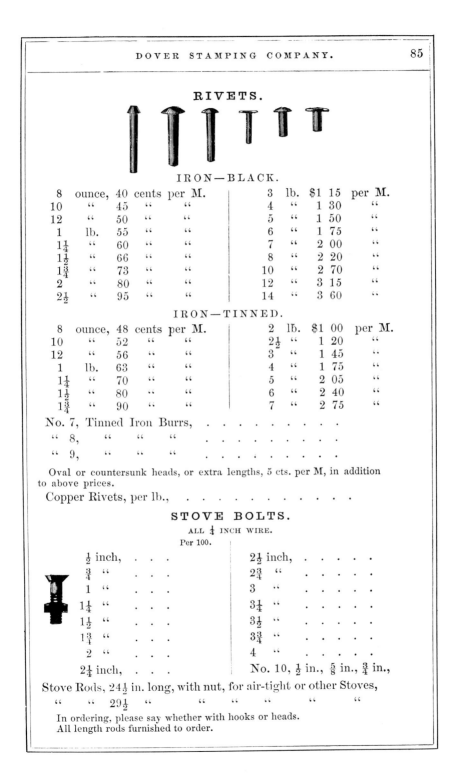

### IRON—BLACK.

| | | | | | | | |
|---|---|---|---|---|---|---|---|
| 8 | ounce, | 40 | cents per M. | 3 | lb. | $1 15 | per M. |
| 10 | " | 45 | " " | 4 | " | 1 30 | " |
| 12 | " | 50 | " " | 5 | " | 1 50 | " |
| 1 | lb. | 55 | " " | 6 | " | 1 75 | " |
| 1¼ | " | 60 | " " | 7 | " | 2 00 | " |
| 1½ | " | 66 | " " | 8 | " | 2 20 | " |
| 1¾ | " | 73 | " " | 10 | " | 2 70 | " |
| 2 | " | 80 | " " | 12 | " | 3 15 | " |
| 2½ | " | 95 | " " | 14 | " | 3 60 | " |

### IRON—TINNED.

| | | | | | | | |
|---|---|---|---|---|---|---|---|
| 8 | ounce, | 48 | cents per M. | 2 | lb. | $1 00 | per M. |
| 10 | " | 52 | " " | 2½ | " | 1 20 | " |
| 12 | " | 56 | " " | 3 | " | 1 45 | " |
| 1 | lb. | 63 | " " | 4 | " | 1 75 | " |
| 1¼ | " | 70 | " " | 5 | " | 2 05 | " |
| 1½ | " | 80 | " " | 6 | " | 2 40 | " |
| 1¾ | " | 90 | " " | 7 | " | 2 75 | " |

No. 7, Tinned Iron Burrs, . . . . . . . . .
" 8,   "   "   "   . . . . . . . .
" 9,   "   "   "   . . . . . . . .

Oval or countersunk heads, or extra lengths, 5 cts. per M, in addition to above prices.

Copper Rivets, per lb., . . . . . . . . . . . .

## STOVE BOLTS.

ALL ¼ INCH WIRE.

Per 100.

| | | | |
|---|---|---|---|
| ½ inch, | . . . | 2½ inch, | . . . . . |
| ¾ " | . . . | 2¾ " | . . . . . |
| 1 " | . . . | 3 " | . . . . . |
| 1¼ " | . . . | 3¼ " | . . . . . |
| 1½ " | . . . | 3½ " | . . . . . |
| 1¾ " | . . . | 3¾ " | . . . . . |
| 2 " | . . . | 4 " | . . . . . |
| 2¼ inch, | . . . | No. 10, ½ in., ⅝ in., ¾ in., | |

Stove Rods, 24½ in. long, with nut, for air-tight or other Stoves,

" " 29½ " " " " " "

In ordering, please say whether with hooks or heads.
All length rods furnished to order.

## PRICES STOVE ORNAMENTS.

| No. 1, . | No. 27, . | No. 52, . | No. 71, . |
|---|---|---|---|
| " 2, . | " 29, . | " 53, . | " 72, . |
| " 3, . | " 31, . | " 54, . | " 73, . |
| " 5, . | " 32', . | " 55, . | " 74, . |
| " 6, . | " 34, . | " 56, . | " 75, . |
| " 7, . | " 35, . | " 57, . | |
| " 8, . | " 38, . | " 58, . | |
| " 10, . | " 40, . | " 59, . | |
| " 11, . | " 41, . | " 60, . | |
| " 12, . | " 42, . | " 61, . | |
| " 14, . | " 43, . | " 62, . | |
| " 15, . | " 44, . | " 63, . | |
| " 16, . | " 45, . | " 64, . | |
| " 18, . | " 46, . | " 65, . | |
| " 20, . | " 47, . | " 66, . | |
| " 21, . | " 48, . | " 67, . | |
| " 22, . | " 49, . | " 68, . | |
| " 23, . | " 50, . | " 69, . | |
| " 24, . | " 51, . | " 70, | |

**RAILING.**
{
No. 5, . . . . . .
" 10, . . . . . .
" 11, . . . . . .
" 14, . . . . . .
" 15, . . . . . .
}

**WROUGHT IRON NUTS.**
{

| Square. | | Thick. | | Hole. | | |
|---|---|---|---|---|---|---|
| 15-32 | x | 5-32 | x | 3-16 | . | . |
| 7-16 | x | 5-32 | x | 7-32 | . | . |
| 7-16 | x | 5-32 | x | 3-16 | . | . |
| 1-2 | x | 3-16 | x | 7-32 | . | . |
| 1-2 | x | 1-4 | x | 7-32 | . | . |

}

## TEA or COFFEE POT KNOBS.

{ Bird, Bright, . . . .

{ Acorn, Bright, . . . .

No. 1, Oval, Black, . .
" 2, " " . .
" 3, " " . .

{ 1 X, Black, . . . . .

{ 2 X, Black, . . . . .

{ 3 X, Black, . . . . .

{ 1 X, Bright, . . . . .

{ 2 X, Bright, . . . . .

{ 3 X, Bright, . . . . .

No. 1, . . . . . . .
" 2, . . . . . . .

100, Round, Plain, . .
200, " " . .
300, " " . .

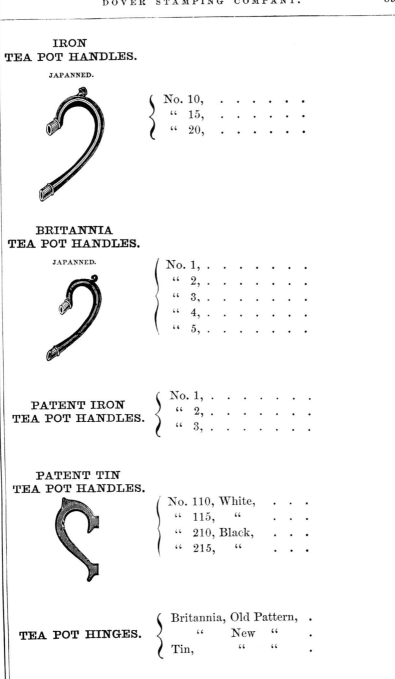

**IRON
TEA POT HANDLES.**

JAPANNED.

No. 10, . . . . . .
" 15, . . . . . .
" 20, . . . . . .

**BRITANNIA
TEA POT HANDLES.**

JAPANNED.

No. 1, . . . . . .
" 2, . . . . . .
" 3, . . . . . .
" 4, . . . . . .
" 5, . . . . . .

**PATENT IRON
TEA POT HANDLES.**

No. 1, . . . . . .
" 2, . . . . . .
" 3, . . . . . .

**PATENT TIN
TEA POT HANDLES.**

No. 110, White, . . .
" 115, " . . .
" 210, Black, . . .
" 215, " . . .

**TEA POT HINGES.**

Britannia, Old Pattern, .
" New " .
Tin, " " .

## BRECKENRIDGE CAN TOPS.

### BRASS.

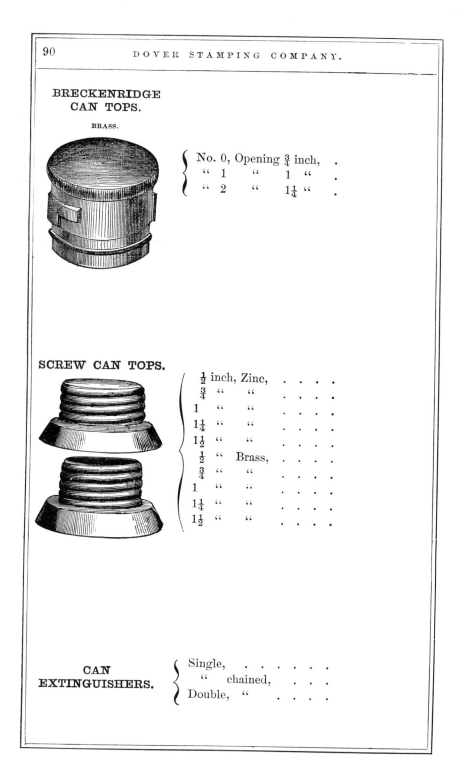

No. 0, Opening $\frac{3}{4}$ inch,   .

" 1    "    1 "    .

" 2    "    $1\frac{1}{4}$ "    .

## SCREW CAN TOPS.

$\frac{1}{2}$ inch, Zinc,   .   .   .   .

$\frac{3}{4}$ "    "    .   .   .   .

1 "    "    .   .   .   .

$1\frac{1}{4}$ "    "    .   .   .   .

$1\frac{1}{2}$ "    "    .   .   .   .

$\frac{1}{2}$ "  Brass,   .   .   .   .

$\frac{3}{4}$ "    "    .   .   .   .

1 "    "    .   .   .   .

$1\frac{1}{4}$ "    "    .   .   .   .

$1\frac{1}{2}$ "    "    .   .   .   .

## CAN EXTINGUISHERS.

Single,   .   .   .   .   .

"   chained,   .   .   .

Double,   "    .   .   .   .

**LAMP EXTINGUISHERS.** {
Single, . . . . . .
" Chained, . . .
Double, " . . .

**OILER COUPLINGS.**
SCREWS AND HOOPS. {
No. 1, . . . . . . .
" 2, . . . . . . .

**OIL SCREWS and HOOPS.**
BLANK OR PIERCED. {
No. 0, . . . . . . .
" 1, Extra, . . . .
" 1, 1 inch, . . . .
" 2, $\frac{7}{8}$ " . . . .
" 3, $\frac{3}{4}$ " . . . .

**OIL SCREWS and HOOPS.**
WITH TUBES. {
No. 1, 2 Tube, 1 in., . .
" 2, 2 " $\frac{7}{8}$ " . .
" 2, 1 " $\frac{7}{8}$ " . .
" 3, 2 " $\frac{3}{4}$ " . .
" 3, 1 " $\frac{3}{4}$ " . .

**TIN OIL TUBES.** {
No. 0, . . . . . . .
" 1, . . . . . . .
" 2, . . . . . . .
" 3, . . . . . . .

**FEEDER SCREWS and HOOPS.** {
No. 1, . . . . . . .
" 2, . . . . . . .

**ALCOHOL BURNERS.** { $\frac{7}{8}$ inch, Large Tube, . .

# MONITOR GAS STOVES,

**(PATENTED MAY 12, 1868.)**

## FOR COOKING AND HEATING.

Unlike all other Gas Stoves, the MONITOR burns with ABSOLUTE PURITY —giving off neither SMOKE or SMELL.

It is not encumbered with perforated plates to become clogged with burning fat or dust. The flame is CLEAR, and burns with a VIVID INTENSITY, but of such PURITY, that polished silver is not soiled when held in it. Vessels may be removed from the stove, and placed upon the tablecloth, without soiling.

## BEEF STEAK OR CHICKEN MAY BE BROILED

*over* or *within* the flame, in the *most perfect manner* — the contact of the flame *imparting no odor whatever.*

Two quarts of water will boil in Six minutes.

Potatoes will bake in Twenly-one minutes.

Biscuit will bake in Nine minutes. And all other cooking is done with the same *perfection* and *rapidity.* The *gas* will cost but *two cents an hour.* The utensils of the Cooking Stove serve admirably for the Monitor. There is no outlay for such articles.

Baking, Boiling, Roasting, Broiling, Frying, Ironing, Washing,— in fact, every labor of a cooking stove is more *perfectly*, more *rapidly*, and more *economically* performed by the Monitor Gas Stove, — and that — without any of the intolerable heat in the room — without the trouble of lighting fires ; without ashes, &c., &c.

The Monitor really does the whole work, which no other Gas Stove can possibly do.

Every Stove warranted.

For the information of Scientific Men, we would state that Sanderson's Patent Gas Burner is an improvement upon the Bunson Patent, whereby is attained an increased temperature, at far less cost, and in much less space.

The peculiar combination of air and gas, in this Stove, brings it under perfect control, and renders it practically available for any purpose where a temperature not above 45.00 degrees Fahrenheit is needed.

---

## DIRECTIONS FOR SETTING AT WORK THE

# MONITOR GAS COOKING STOVE.

Be sure of an AMPLE SUPPLY OF GAS, and see that the connecting pipe is of *sufficient size,* and the *Stop Cocks clear* — to admit it. Connect with either flexible or metal pipe.

Turn on a *full head* of gas, and light at top of burner. *There must be no flame below the* TOP *of the burner.* If the gas be poor, and supply insufficient, the blaze *may* drop to the bottom, inside of the burner, and burn with a flame of less intensity — not unlike that of a burner for *lighting* purposes ; in which case, *turn off* the gas, and begin again. If it still persists in dropping down — and burning below the top — the *sides* of the top of the burner must be pressed together — a very little — just enough to remedy the difficulty.

Any flame like that used for lighting purposes *will not do* — for lack of heat.

The RIGHT FLAME is BLUE at the BASE — and CHERRY RED at the TOP — the BLUE part reaching to within about a half inch of the article to be heated.

The quality, richness and pressure of gas being different in different places — the adjustment of the burner must be left to him who uses it. All are made to work perfectly with Boston gas. By a little attention, they will work *anywhere.*

☞ *See that the Burner Regulations of the Gas Company are complied with in setting this Stove at work.*

The estimates are based upon gas at $3.25 per 1000 feet.

Satisfactory testimonials and references sent to those who require them.

## WINSHIP'S REFRIGERATOR.

**SELF-VENTILATING.**

| No. | Width. Inches. | Depth. Inches. | Height. Inches. | Walnut, Oak, &c. | Double Doors and Chambers. |
|---|---|---|---|---|---|
| 2 | 31 | 22 | 43 | $31 00 | |
| 3 | 34 | 25 | 44 | 37 00 | |
| 4 | 39 | 26 | 47 | 44 00 | $50 00 |
| 5 | 43 | 27 | 51 | 50 00 | 60 00 |
| 6 | 50 | 32 | 60 | | 100 00 |
| 7 | 61 | 36 | 74 | | |

INSIDE VIEW, EXHIBITING

VENTILATING CURRENT.

This Refrigerator is offered to the public as an EFFICIENT DOMESTIC SANITARY REFORM. *Unventilated Ice-chests* destroy the purity of food and *induce* decomposition; and it is conceded by Physicians that provisions are rendered *very unwholesome* by being confined in an apartment in which the air is not *constantly and effectually changed*, and the health of many families has suffered in consequence. To prove this, we need only allude to the moisture deposited on articles of food placed therein, which *promotes decay;* and the offensive smell pervading them is a sure indication of the presence of this poisonous tendency. *Dryness* is as requisite as cold, to prevent decay, and *cannot* be secured in an air-tight Refrigerator.

"Winship's Patent Self-Ventilating Refrigerator combines all the qualities to be desired; is constructed on sound principles of philosophy, and is practically, as well as theoretically, right." — *From the Boston Medical and Surgical Journal,* June 23, 1859.

We refer for critical opinions regarding it, to the FIRST PRINCIPLES OF PHILOSOPHY," by PROF. SILLIMAN, JR., of Yale, and, to " CHEMICAL PHYSICS," by PROF. COOKE, of Harvard, scientific text-books of the highest authority, both of which instance its operation as an adroit and *perfect* adaptation of the laws of ventilation to domestic economy. The *"Boston Medical and Surgical Journal"* urges its general adoption on *hygienic* and economic grounds.

The temperature is *always uniform.* The air never becomes *stagnant.* Access to the ice is had without disturbing the provision-chamber. Articles of *different flavors* cannot *impregnate* each other. *Milk, delicate Fruits, and Meats,* can be *preserved much longer* than in any other Refrigerator. All who value *health* and *pure food*, are advised to give this article a trial.

No household, however limited in means, should be without a WINSHIP REFRIGERATOR. Economy — to say nothing of the luxury — demands the investment of the small amount required to purchase one. Pamphlets containing a full discussion of its merits, together with the indorsement of all the prominent scientific men in the country, forwarded to all who wish it.

☞ Dealers promptly supplied.

# DOVER STAMPING CO.,
### *88 & 90 North Street, Boston,*
MANUFACTURERS AND AGENTS FOR

NEW ENGLAND, NEW BRUNSWICK, NOVA SCOTIA, P. E. ISLAND and the CANADAS.

## ICE KING FREEZER.

| | | |
|---|---|---|
| 2 Quart, | . . . . . . . . . | . $3 00 |
| 3 " | . . . . . . . . | . 4 00 |
| 4 " | . . . . . . . . | . 5 00 |
| 6 " | . . . . . . . . | . 6 50 |
| 8 " | . . . . . . . . | . 8 00 |
| 14 " | . . . . . . . . | . 12 00 |
| 23 " | . . . . . . . . | . 15 00 |

### THIS FREEZER

is warranted to

## Freeze Cream in as little time as good Cream can be Frozen!

by any economical process known.

Any one with ORDINARY ABILITY can do this WITHOUT THE AID OF PRACTICAL SKILL.

### FULL DIRECTIONS ACCOMPANY EACH FREEZER

for mixing cream and freezing it.

With the ICE KING a few quarts of Ice Cream can be produced in as little time as is taken to make a bowl of Lemonade, while any domestic may become, in a few minutes, competent to do it all.

These facts obviate the objections to home-made Ice Cream, and recommend the ICE KING to

UNIVERSAL FAMILY USE.

**TACKS.**

{
3 ounce, . .
4 " . .
6 " . .
8 " . .
10 " . .
12 " . .
14 " . .
16 " . .
18 " . .
20 " . .
}

**CARPET TACKS.**
LARGE IRON HEADS.

{
8 ounce, . .
10 " . .
}

**CARPET TACKS.**
LEATHER HEADS.

{
100 in paper, .
144 " .
}

**COPPER TACKS.**
IN 1 LB. PAPERS.

{
$\frac{1}{2}$ inch, . . .
$\frac{5}{8}$ " . . .
$\frac{3}{4}$ " . . .
1 " . . .
}

**IRON JACK CHAIN.**

{
No. 9, . . .
" 10, . . .
" 11, . . .
" 12, . . .
" 13, . . .
" 14, . . .
" 15, . . .
" 16, . . .
" 17, . . .
" 18, . . .
" 19, . . .
" 20, . . .
" 22, . . .
" 22, Brass,
}

**FORGED
SAUCE PAN HANDLES.**

TINNED.

No. 1, 5 inch, .
" 2, 6½ " .
" 3, 7½ " .
" 4, 8½ " .
" 5, 9½ " .

**FORGED
SAUCE PAN HANDLES.**

BLACK.

No. 1, 5 inch, .
" 2, 6½ " .
" 3, 7½ " .
" 4, 8½ " .
" 5, 9½ " .

**FRENCH
SAUCE PAN HANDLES.**

TINNED.

No. 1, 6 inch, .
" 2, 7 " .
" 3, 8 " .
" 4, 9 " .
" 5, 10 " .
" 6, 11 " .

**FRENCH
SAUCE PAN HANDLES.**

BLACK.

No. 1, 6 inch, .
" 2, 7 " .
" 3, 8 " .
" 4, 9 " .
" 5, 10 " .
" 6, 11 " .

**SOCKET
SAUCE PAN HANDLES.**

TINNED.

6 inch, . . .
7 " . . .
8 " . . .
9 " . . .
10 " . . .
12 " . . .
14 " . . .

## PATENT UNION BOX COFFEE MILL.

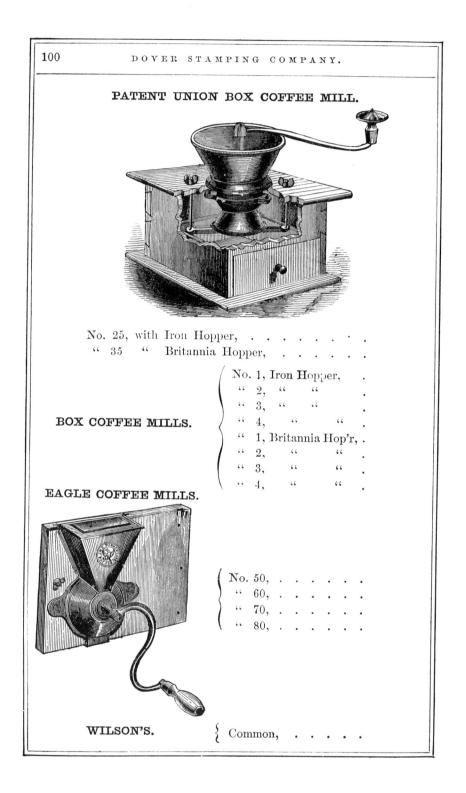

No. 25, with Iron Hopper, . . . . . . . .

" 35 " Britannia Hopper, . . . . . .

**BOX COFFEE MILLS.**

No. 1, Iron Hopper, .
" 2, " " .
" 3, " " .
" 4, " " .
" 1, Britannia Hop'r, .
" 2, " " .
" 3, " " .
" 4, " " .

**EAGLE COFFEE MILLS.**

No. 50, . . . . . . .
" 60, . . . . . .
" 70, . . . . . .
" 80, . . . . . .

**WILSON'S.**  Common, . . . . . .

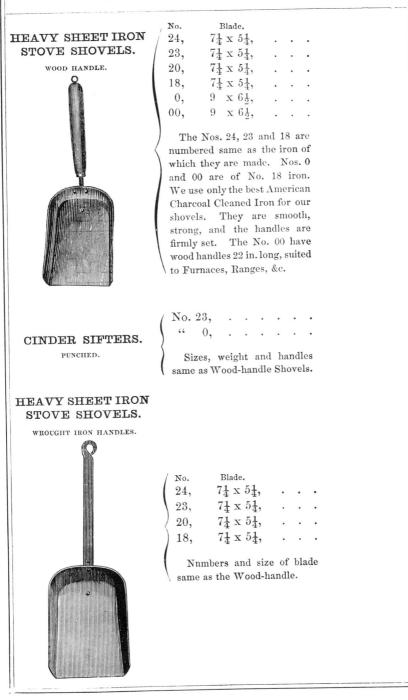

## HEAVY SHEET IRON STOVE SHOVELS.

### WOOD HANDLE.

| No. | Blade. | | |
|---|---|---|---|
| 24, | $7\frac{1}{4}$ x $5\frac{1}{4}$, | . . . |
| 23, | $7\frac{1}{4}$ x $5\frac{1}{4}$, | . . . |
| 20, | $7\frac{1}{4}$ x $5\frac{1}{4}$, | . . . |
| 18, | $7\frac{1}{4}$ x $5\frac{1}{4}$, | . . . |
| 0, | 9 x $6\frac{1}{2}$, | . . . |
| 00, | 9 x $6\frac{1}{2}$, | . . . |

The Nos. 24, 23 and 18 are numbered same as the iron of which they are made. Nos. 0 and 00 are of No. 18 iron. We use only the best American Charcoal Cleaned Iron for our shovels. They are smooth, strong, and the handles are firmly set. The No. 00 have wood handles 22 in. long, suited to Furnaces, Ranges, &c.

## CINDER SIFTERS.

### PUNCHED.

No. 23, . . . . . .
" 0, . . . . . .

Sizes, weight and handles same as Wood-handle Shovels.

## HEAVY SHEET IRON STOVE SHOVELS.

### WROUGHT IRON HANDLES.

| No. | Blade. | | |
|---|---|---|---|
| 24, | $7\frac{1}{4}$ x $5\frac{1}{4}$, | . . . |
| 23, | $7\frac{1}{4}$ x $5\frac{1}{4}$, | . . . |
| 20, | $7\frac{1}{4}$ x $5\frac{1}{4}$, | . . . |
| 18, | $7\frac{1}{4}$ x $5\frac{1}{4}$, | . . . |

Numbers and size of blade same as the Wood-handle.

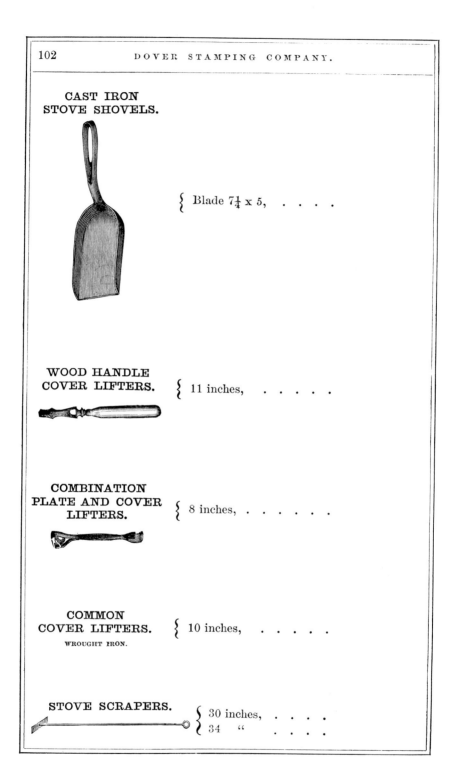

**CAST IRON
STOVE SHOVELS.**

$\{$ Blade $7\frac{1}{4}$ x 5, . . . .

**WOOD HANDLE
COVER LIFTERS.**

$\{$ 11 inches, . . . . .

**COMBINATION
PLATE AND COVER
LIFTERS.**

$\{$ 8 inches, . . . . . .

**COMMON
COVER LIFTERS.**
WROUGHT IRON.

$\{$ 10 inches, . . . . .

**STOVE SCRAPERS.**

$\{$ 30 inches, . . . .
$\{$ 34 " . . . .

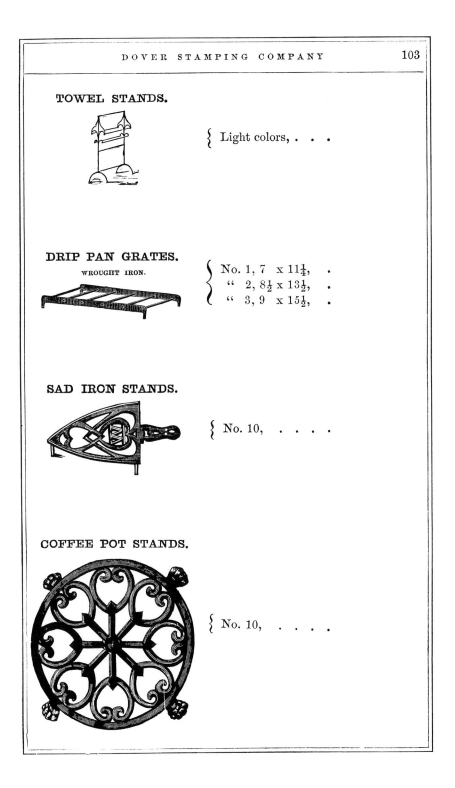

## TOWEL STANDS.

{ Light colors, . . .

## DRIP PAN GRATES.

WROUGHT IRON.

{ No. 1, 7  x 11¼,  .
" 2, 8½ x 13½,  .
" 3, 9  x 15½,  .

## SAD IRON STANDS.

{ No. 10,  . . . .

## COFFEE POT STANDS.

{ No. 10,  . . . .

**SHOVEL and TONGS.**

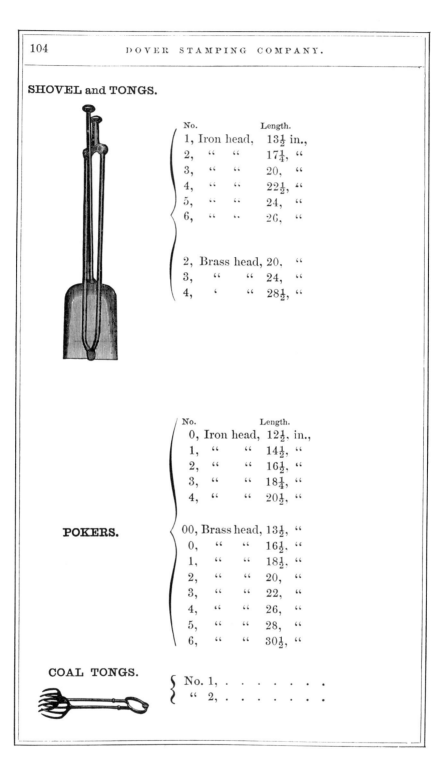

| No. | | | Length. |
|---|---|---|---|
| 1, Iron head, | | | 13½ in., |
| 2, | " | " | 17¼, " |
| 3, | " | " | 20, " |
| 4, | " | " | 22½, " |
| 5, | " | " | 24, " |
| 6, | " | " | 26, " |
| | | | |
| 2, Brass head, | | | 20, " |
| 3, | " | " | 24, " |
| 4, | ' | " | 28½, " |

**POKERS.**

| No. | | | Length. |
|---|---|---|---|
| 0, Iron head, | | | 12½, in., |
| 1, | " | " | 14½, " |
| 2, | " | " | 16½, " |
| 3, | " | " | 18¼, " |
| 4, | " | " | 20½, " |
| | | | |
| 00, Brass head, | | | 13½, " |
| 0, | " | " | 16½, " |
| 1, | " | " | 18½, " |
| 2, | " | " | 20, " |
| 3, | " | " | 22, " |
| 4, | " | " | 26, " |
| 5, | " | " | 28, " |
| 6, | " | " | 30½, " |

**COAL TONGS.**

No. 1, . . . . . . . .
" 2, . . . . . . . .

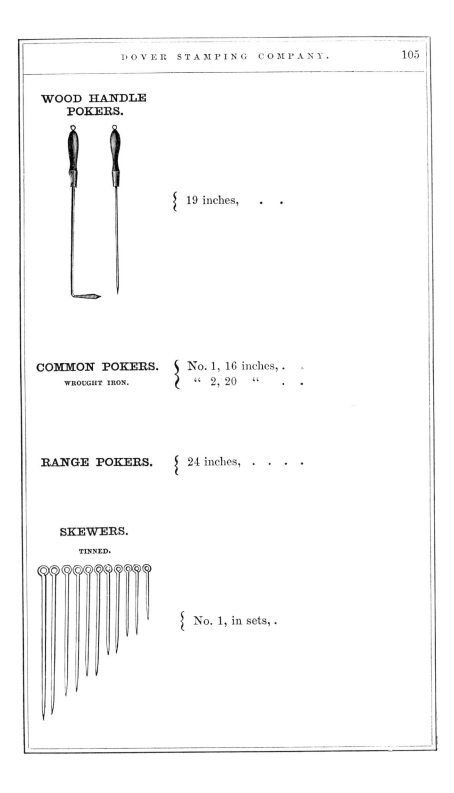

**WOOD HANDLE POKERS.**

{ 19 inches, . .

**COMMON POKERS.**
WROUGHT IRON.

{ No. 1, 16 inches, . .
{ " 2, 20 " . .

**RANGE POKERS.**

{ 24 inches, . . . .

**SKEWERS.**
TINNED.

{ No. 1, in sets, .

## SAD IRONS.

### D. S. CO. PATTERN.

{
No. 1, from 5 to 10, .
" 2, " 5 " 10, .
Finished in the highest
Style. Superior quality.

### B. & D. PATTERN.

{ Sizes from 5 to 10, .

## CHARCOAL IRONS.

{
With   Shield, . .
Without " . .
For Tailors, . . .

## POLISHING IRONS.

### D. S. CO. PATTERN.

{ One size, . . . .

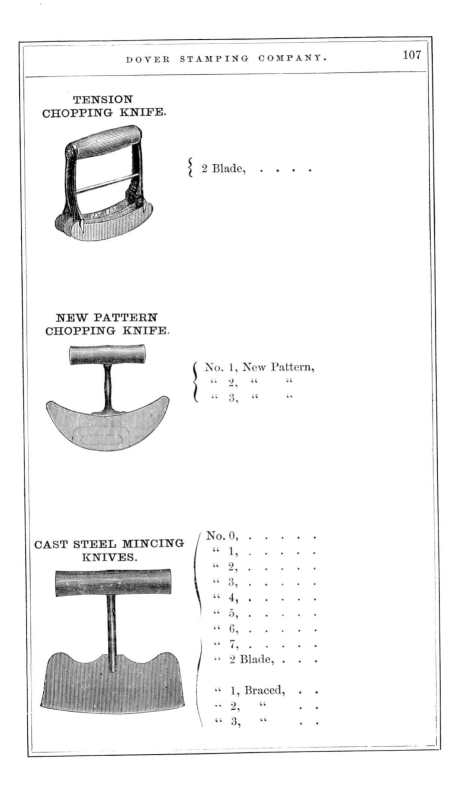

**TENSION CHOPPING KNIFE.**

{ 2 Blade, . . . .

**NEW PATTERN CHOPPING KNIFE.**

{ No. 1, New Pattern,
  " 2,    "     "
  " 3,    "     "

**CAST STEEL MINCING KNIVES.**

No. 0, . . . . .
  " 1, . . . . .
  " 2, . . . . .
  " 3, . . . . .
  " 4, . . . . .
  " 5, . . . . .
  " 6, . . . . .
  " 7, . . . . .
  " 2 Blade, . . .

  " 1, Braced, . .
  " 2,   "     . .
  " 3,   "     . .

KITCHEN KNIVES.  { 3 inches, . . . .
                 { 3½  "    . . . .

MEAT KNIVES.     { C. S. Pointed, . . .

BREAD KNIVES.    { C. S. Round points, .

BUTCHER KNIVES.  { No. 1, . . . . .

SINK CLEANERS.   { One size, . . . .

KNIFE CLEANERS.  { One size, . . . .

TACK HAMMERS.    { No. 10, . . . . .
                 {  "  15, . . . . .
                 {  "  25, . . . . .
                 {  "  35, . . . . .

## MUNROE'S
## PATENT MELTING LADLES.

MUNROE'S
PATENT
JUNE 14.
1864.

{ No. 1, . . . .

**SPRING BALANCES.**

{
No.
60, Extra Light,
61, . . . . .
81, (Frary's,) .
170, Round, . .

## COMMON
## MELTING LADLES.

{ 4 inch, . . . .

**SCREW EYES.**

{

**PASTE JAGGERS.**

WOOD WHEEL.

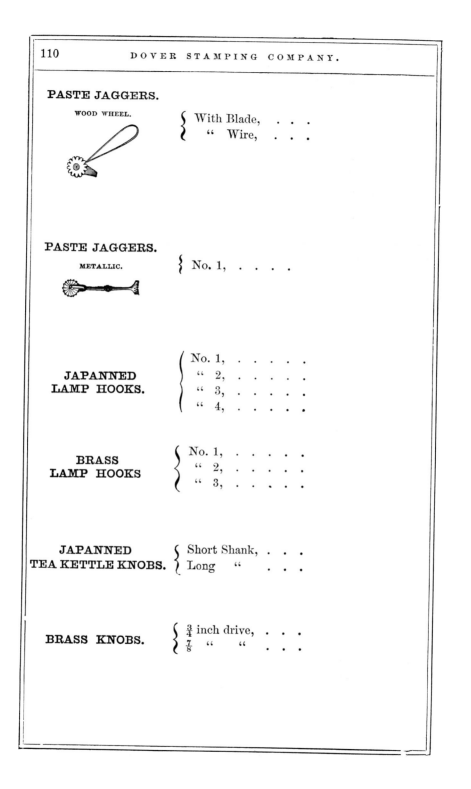

} With Blade,  . . .
   "  Wire,  . . .

**PASTE JAGGERS.**

METALLIC.

} No. 1,  . . . .

**JAPANNED
LAMP HOOKS.**

{ No. 1,  . . . . .
  " 2,  . . . . .
  " 3,  . . . . .
  " 4,  . . . . .

**BRASS
LAMP HOOKS**

} No. 1,  . . . . .
  " 2,  . . . . .
  " 3,  . . . . .

**JAPANNED
TEA KETTLE KNOBS.**

} Short Shank,  . . .
Long   "   . . .

**BRASS  KNOBS.**

} $\frac{3}{4}$ inch drive,  . . .
$\frac{7}{8}$  "   "  . . .

**EXCELSIOR MOPS.**

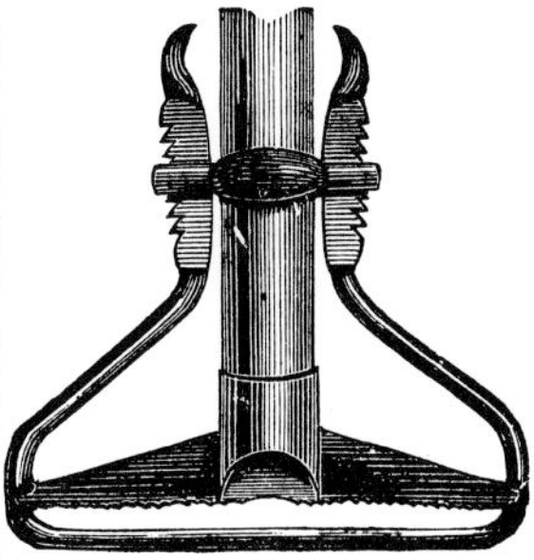

{ Plain, . . . . .
{ Coppered, . . . . .

**WOOD SAWS.** { With Frame, . . .

**CLOTHES PINS.** { 5 gro. boxes, . . .

**ICE PICKS.**
{ Small, . . . . .
{ Large, . . . . .
{ Patent, Slide, . . .

**ICE MALLETS.**
{ No. 1, . . . . .
{ " 2, . . . . .

**PAIL WOODS.**

IN BBLS. OR 500 BOXES.

{ No. 1, Black, . . .
{ " 2, " . . .
{ " 3, " . . .
{ " 4, " . . .
{ " 4, White, . . .

## HERSEY'S PATENT
## DOUBLE ACTION APPLE PARER.

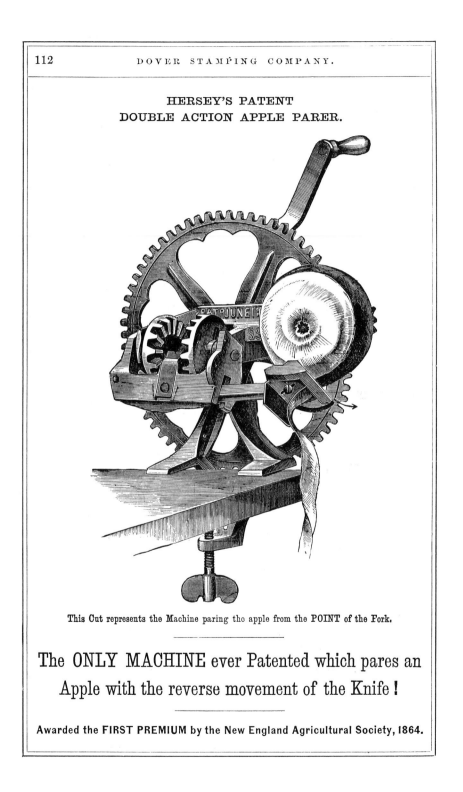

This Cut represents the Machine paring the apple from the POINT of the Fork.

---

# The ONLY MACHINE ever Patented which pares an Apple with the reverse movement of the Knife !

---

**Awarded the FIRST PREMIUM by the New England Agricultural Society, 1864.**

# SUPERIORITY OF THIS MACHINE

## OVER ALL OTHERS!

### 1st    It is the most rapid worker.

By one and a half turns of the crank it pares the apple and carries the knife out of the way, so that the apple may be removed without danger of cutting or bruising the hand by coming in contact with any part of the machine. By another turn and a half of the crank the knife is *reversed* and *pares back to its original position*, and this *without reversing* the movement of the crank; thus paring *two* apples with *only three* turns of the crank, which is several times less than is required by any other machine.

### 2d.   It is the most cleanly Machine.

By the peculiar construction and position of the knife, it is impossible for the parings and juice of the apple to come in contact with the bearings and gear of the machine, thereby avoiding the disagreeable gumming up and dirt incident to all other machines, and no oil can come in contact with the fruit. By placing the machine on the corner of the table or bench *all the parings* will fall clear of the machine into any recepticle which may be placed for them.

### 3d   It is the most durable Machine.

There are no short bearings that are subject to much friction, as is almost universally the case in other machines. Every bearing can be thoroughly and easily oiled, and as the juice of the apple cannot get to the bearings to destroy the oil, a large proportion of the friction incident to all other machines is avoided.

## COAL HODS.

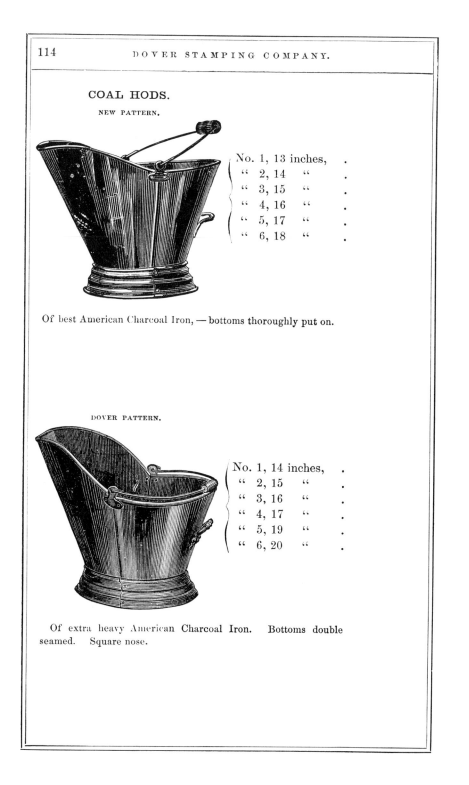

No. 1, 13 inches,   .
" 2, 14   "        .
" 3, 15   "        .
" 4, 16   "        .
" 5, 17   "        .
" 6, 18   "        .

Of best American Charcoal Iron, — bottoms thoroughly put on.

DOVER PATTERN.

No. 1, 14 inches,   .
" 2, 15   "         .
" 3, 16   "         .
" 4, 17   "         .
" 5, 19   "         .
" 6, 20   "         .

Of extra heavy American Charcoal Iron.    Bottoms double seamed.    Square nose.

## SHIELD HODS.

RICHLY ORNAMENTED.

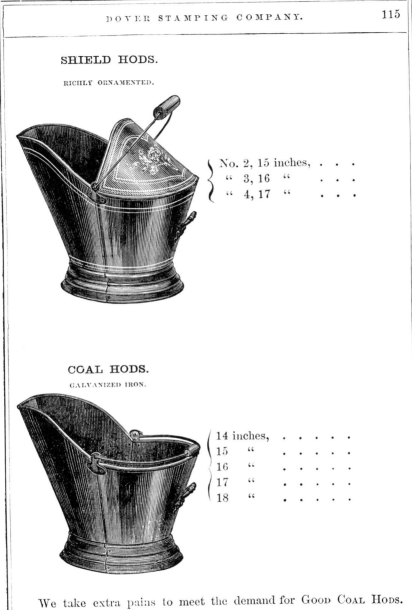

No. 2, 15 inches, . . .
" 3, 16 " . . .
" 4, 17 " . . .

## COAL HODS.

GALVANIZED IRON.

14 inches, . . . . .
15 " . . . . .
16 " . . . . .
17 " . . . . .
18 " . . . . .

We take extra pains to meet the demand for GOOD COAL HODS.
Hods of our make are SMOOTHLY FINISHED AND DURABLE.

## PATENT TUNNEL HODS.

No. 2, 15 inch  .  .  .  .  .  .  .  .  .  .
" 3, 16 "  .  .  .  .  .  .  .  .  .
" 4, 17 "  .  .  .  .  .  .  .  .  .
" 5, 18 "  .  .  .  .  .  .  .  .  .
" 6, 19 "  .  .  .  .  .  .  .  .  .
" 7, 21 "  .  .  .  .  .  .  .  .  .

This Coal Hod is constructed for the greater convenience of filling through the side doors of Parlor Stoves and Base Burners, and all Stoves to be filled at the top.

The angle of the Tunnel is such that when the Hod is tipped sufficient to permit the coal of itself to pass freely in,

### THE NOZZLE STANDS UPRIGHT WITH THE DOOR,

leaving no opening around it for the coal to fall through upon the floor. The most desirable Tunnel Coal Hod made.

# DOVER STAMPING CO.,
## BOSTON.

## CAST IRON
## DAMPERS and RODS.

| | | | | | |
|---|---|---|---|---|---|
| 4 inches, | • | • | • | • | |
| 4½ " | • | • | • | • | • |
| 5 " | • | • | • | • | • |
| 5½ " | • | • | • | • | • |
| 6 " | • | • | • | • | • |
| 7 " | • | • | • | • | • |

## DAMPER RODS
## ONLY.

| | | | | | |
|---|---|---|---|---|---|
| 4 inches, | • | • | • | • | |
| 4½ " | • | • | • | • | • |
| 5 " | • | • | • | • | • |
| 5½ " | • | • | • | • | • |
| 6 " | • | • | • | • | • |
| 7 " | • | • | • | • | • |

## PATENT
## SPRING DAMPER.

| | | | | |
|---|---|---|---|---|
| 4 inches, | • | • | • | • |
| 4½ " | | • | • | • |
| 5 " | | • | • | • |
| 5½ " | | • | • | • |
| 6 " | | • | • | • |
| 7 " | | • | • | • |
| 8 " | | • | • | • |

The spring attached to the spindle holds this Damper exactly in place, *at any angle.* The hole punched for the Spindle receives the spring—involving neither trouble or expense. Does not get out of order. It is the best Damper made.

## HOWARD'S PAT.
## RATCHET DAMPER.

| | | | | |
|---|---|---|---|---|
| 5 inches, | • | • | • | • |
| 5½ " | • | • | • | • |
| 6 " | • | • | • | • |
| 7 " | • | • | • | • |
| 8 " | • | • | • | • |

## CAST IRON
## PIPE COLLARS.

$\left\{\begin{array}{l}\text{4}\frac{1}{2} \text{ inch opening,} \quad . \\ \text{5 \quad `` \quad `` \quad .} \\ \text{5}\frac{1}{2} \text{ `` \quad `` \quad .} \\ \text{6 \quad `` \quad `` \quad .} \\ \text{7 \quad `` \quad ``} \end{array}\right.$

## ASH DOOR.

$\left\{\begin{array}{l}\text{Small, 10 x 12}\frac{1}{2}\text{, . .} \\ \text{Large, . . . . . .}\end{array}\right.$

## BOILER DOORS.
#### WITH GRATES.

$\left\{\begin{array}{l}\text{10 x 12}\frac{1}{2}\text{, . . . .} \\ \text{Grates only, . . .}\end{array}\right.$

# CAST IRON SINKS.

WITH CESSPOOLS.

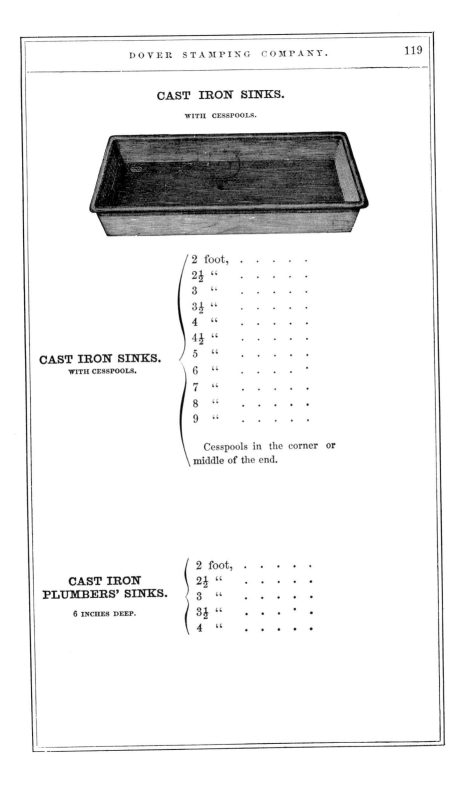

**CAST IRON SINKS.**
WITH CESSPOOLS.

2 foot, . . . . .
2½ " . . . . .
3 " . . . . .
3½ " . . . . .
4 " . . . . .
4½ " . . . . .
5 " . . . . .
6 " . . . . .
7 " . . . . .
8 " . . . . .
9 " . . . . .

Cesspools in the corner or middle of the end.

**CAST IRON PLUMBERS' SINKS.**
6 INCHES DEEP.

2 foot, . . . . .
2½ " . . . . .
3 " . . . . .
3½ " . . . . .
4 " . . . . .

## WATERMAN'S
## PATENT BAKE PANS.

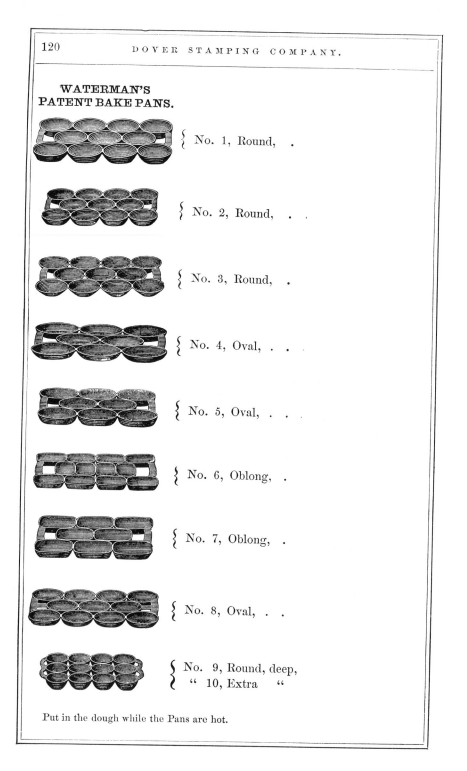

} No. 1, Round,   .

} No. 2, Round,   . .

} No. 3, Round,   .

} No. 4, Oval, . . .

} No. 5, Oval, . . .

} No. 6, Oblong,  .

} No. 7, Oblong,  .

} No. 8, Oval, . .

} No.  9, Round, deep,
  " 10, Extra    "

Put in the dough while the Pans are hot.

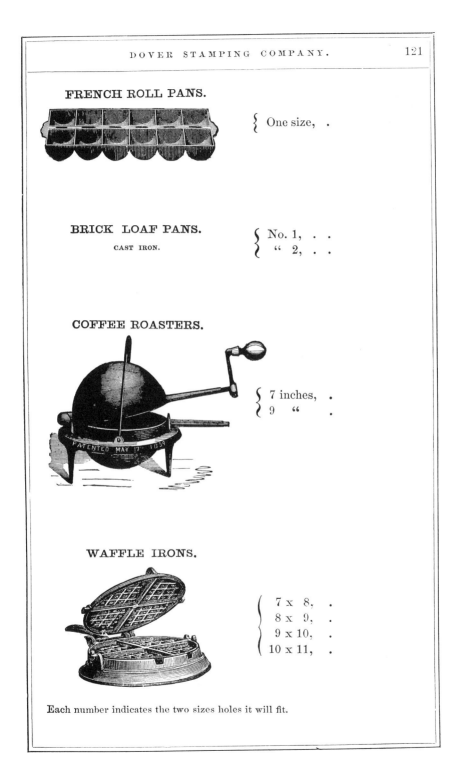

## FRENCH ROLL PANS.

{ One size, .

## BRICK LOAF PANS.

### CAST IRON.

{ No. 1, . .
{ " 2, . .

## COFFEE ROASTERS.

{ 7 inches, .
{ 9 " .

## WAFFLE IRONS.

{ 7 x 8, .
{ 8 x 9, .
{ 9 x 10, .
{ 10 x 11, .

Each number indicates the two sizes holes it will fit.

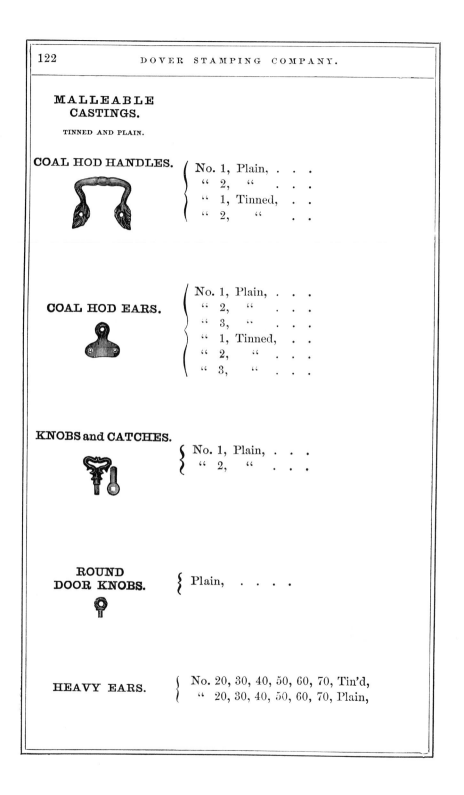

## MALLEABLE CASTINGS.

TINNED AND PLAIN.

**COAL HOD HANDLES.**

No. 1, Plain, . . .
" 2,  "  . . .
" 1, Tinned, . .
" 2,   "   . .

**COAL HOD EARS.**

No. 1, Plain, . . .
" 2,  "  . . .
" 3,  "  . . .
" 1, Tinned, . .
" 2,   "   . .
" 3,   "   . .

**KNOBS and CATCHES.**

No. 1, Plain, . . .
" 2,   "   . . .

**ROUND DOOR KNOBS.**

Plain, . . . .

**HEAVY EARS.**

No. 20, 30, 40, 50, 60, 70, Tin'd,
"  20, 30, 40, 50, 60, 70, Plain,

## MALLEABLE CASTINGS.

TINNED AND PLAIN.

**CAN HANDLES.**
{ No. 1, Plain, . . .
" 2, " . . .
No. 1, Tinned, . .
" 2, " . . .

**TUREEN HANDLES.**
{ 100 Tinned, . . .
200 " . . . .
300 " . . . .

**TUREEN TOP HANDLES.**
{ Tinned, . . .

**TOILET HANDLES.**
{ One Size, . . . .

**URN FEET.**
{ Tinned. . . . .

**DRAINER FEET.**
{ No. 1, Tinned, . .
" 2, " . .

PARTICULAR ATTENTION IS CALLED TO

# THE RELIANCE WRINGER,

Which we have adopted Exclusively for our Trade.

It combines all the qualities of a

## FIRST-CLASS WRINGER,

STRENGTH,

SIMPLICITY,

DURABILITY.

WITH OR WITHOUT COG WHEELS.

Its SPECIAL MERIT OVER ALL OTHERS is in its

**SPIRAL GEAR**

AND

**PATENT**

## KEYED ROLLS.

Great strength is given to the rubber of these Patent Rolls, by an internal support of heavy Duck, to which it is vulcanized — the Duck being keyed in the grooves of the shaft by strong iron rods, which prevent the rubber turning on the shaft.

THE ROLLS ARE

## WARRANTED NOT TO TWIST OFF.

☞ It wrings the FINEST or COARSEST article without injury.

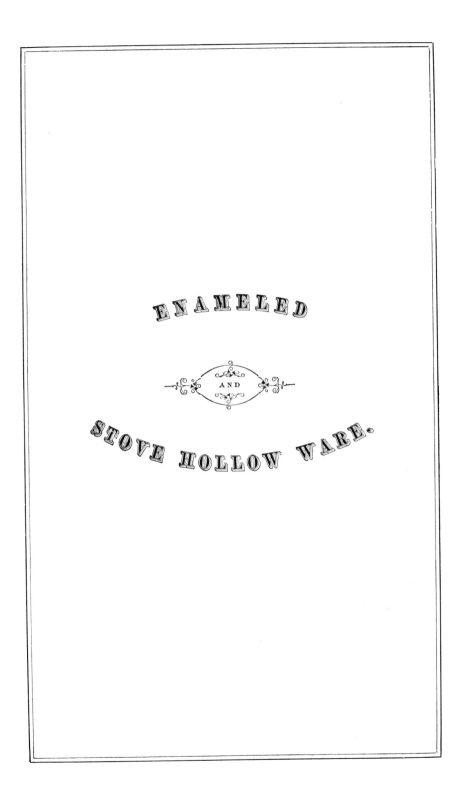

ENAMELED

AND

STOVE HOLLOW WARE.

## ENAMELED HOLLOW WARES.

TINNED, SAME PRICE.

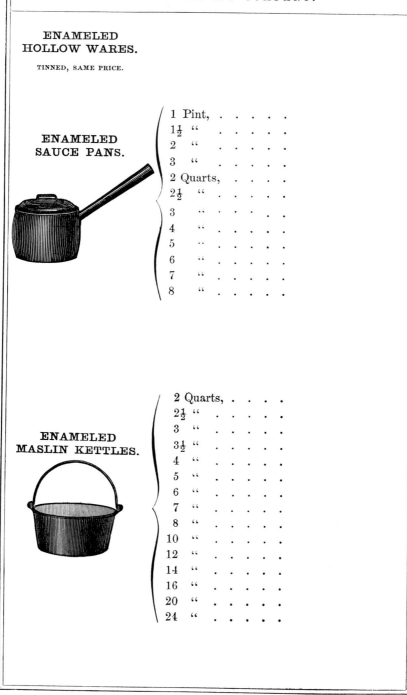

### ENAMELED SAUCE PANS.

| | |
|---|---|
| 1 Pint, | . . . . . |
| 1½ " | . . . . |
| 2 " | . . . . |
| 3 " | . . . . |
| 2 Quarts, | . . . |
| 2½ " | . . . . |
| 3 " | . . . . |
| 4 " | . . . . |
| 5 " | . . . . |
| 6 " | . . . . |
| 7 " | . . . . |
| 8 " | . . . |

### ENAMELED MASLIN KETTLES.

| | |
|---|---|
| 2 Quarts, | . . . . |
| 2½ " | . . . . |
| 3 " | . . . . |
| 3½ " | . . . . |
| 4 " | . . . . |
| 5 " | . . . . |
| 6 " | . . . . |
| 7 " | . . . . |
| 8 " | . . . . |
| 10 " | . . . . |
| 12 " | . . . . |
| 14 " | . . . . |
| 16 " | . . . . |
| 20 " | . . . . |
| 24 " | . . . . . |

## ENAMELED HOLLOW WARES.

TINNED, SAME PRICE.

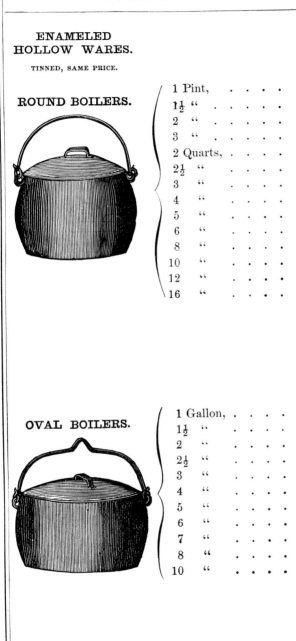

### ROUND BOILERS.

| | |
|---|---|
| 1 Pint, | . . . . |
| 1½ " | . . . . |
| 2 " | . . . . |
| 3 " | . . . . |
| 2 Quarts, | . . . |
| 2½ " | . . . . |
| 3 " | . . . . |
| 4 " | . . . . |
| 5 " | . . . . |
| 6 " | . . . . |
| 8 " | . . . . |
| 10 " | . . . . |
| 12 " | . . . . |
| 16 " | . . . . |

### OVAL BOILERS.

| | |
|---|---|
| 1 Gallon, | . . . |
| 1½ " | . . . . |
| 2 " | . . . . |
| 2½ " | . . . . |
| 3 " | . . . . |
| 4 " | . . . . |
| 5 " | . . . . |
| 6 " | . . . . |
| 7 " | . . . . |
| 8 " | . . . . |
| 10 " | . . . . |

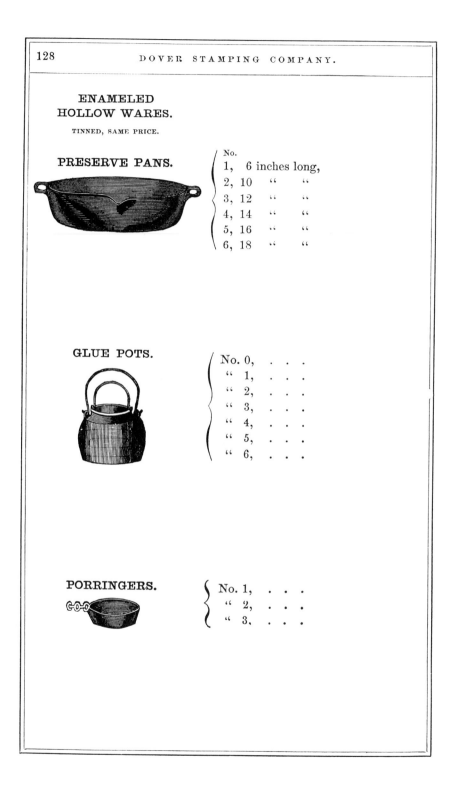

## ENAMELED
## HOLLOW WARES.

TINNED, SAME PRICE.

**PRESERVE PANS.**

No.
1,   6 inches long,
2, 10  "    "
3, 12  "    "
4, 14  "    "
5, 16  "    "
6, 18  "    "

**GLUE POTS.**

No. 0,   .   .   .
 "   1,   .   .   .
 "   2,   .   .   .
 "   3,   .   .   .
 "   4,   .   .   .
 "   5,   .   .   .
 "   6,   .   .   .

**PORRINGERS.**

No. 1,   .   .   .
 "   2,   .   .   .
 "   3,   .   .   .

# HOLLOW WARES.

## SHOAL SCOTCH BOWLS.

JAPANNED.

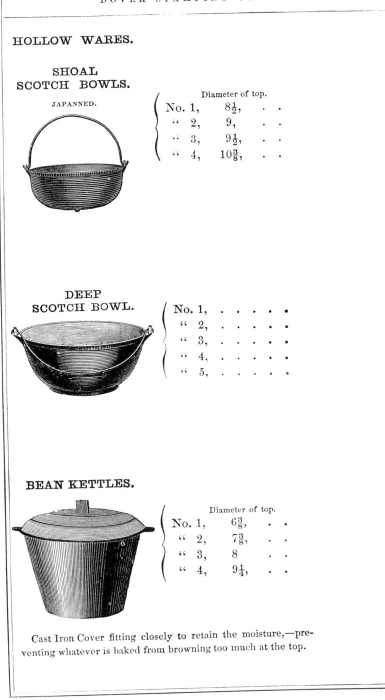

Diameter of top.

| | | |
|---|---|---|
| No. 1, | $8\frac{1}{2}$, | . . |
| " 2, | 9, | . . |
| " 3, | $9\frac{1}{2}$, | . . |
| " 4, | $10\frac{3}{8}$, | . . |

## DEEP SCOTCH BOWL.

| | |
|---|---|
| No. 1, | . . . . . |
| " 2, | . . . . . |
| " 3, | . . . . . |
| " 4, | . . . . . |
| " 5, | . . . . ∘ |

## BEAN KETTLES.

Diameter of top.

| | | |
|---|---|---|
| No. 1, | $6\frac{3}{8}$, | . . |
| " 2, | $7\frac{3}{8}$, | . . |
| " 3, | 8 | . . |
| " 4, | $9\frac{1}{4}$, | . . |

Cast Iron Cover fitting closely to retain the moisture,—preventing whatever is baked from browning too much at the top.

# HOLLOW WARE.

## HIGH PANS.
### JAPANNED.

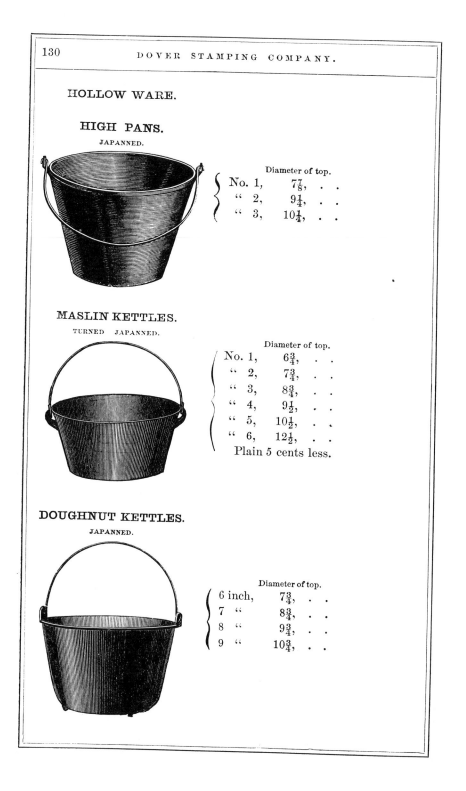

Diameter of top.

No. 1,      7⅞, . .
"   2,      9¼, . .
"   3,     10¼, . .

## MASLIN KETTLES.
### TURNED   JAPANNED.

Diameter of top.

No. 1,      6¾, . .
"   2,      7¾, . .
"   3,      8¾, . .
"   4,      9½, . .
"   5,     10½, . .
"   6,     12½, . .
Plain 5 cents less.

## DOUGHNUT KETTLES.
### JAPANNED.

Diameter of top.

6 inch,      7¾, . .
7  "      8¾, . .
8  "      9¾, . .
9  "     10¾, . .

## SIZES OF OUR COVERS,

### To fit Stove Hollow Ware of different Makers.

#### PRATT & WENTWORTH.

Pots.  Kettles.

$\frac{9\frac{1}{4}}{6}$ $\frac{9\frac{1}{2}}{6\frac{1}{2}}$ $\frac{9\frac{3}{4}}{7}$ $\frac{10\frac{3}{4}}{7\frac{1}{2}}$ $\frac{10\frac{3}{4}}{8}$ $\frac{11}{8\frac{1}{2}}$ $\frac{11}{9}$ $\frac{13}{9\frac{1}{2}}$ $\frac{}{10}$ in.  $\frac{8\frac{3}{4}}{6}$ $\frac{9\frac{1}{4}}{6\frac{1}{2}}$ $\frac{9\frac{1}{4}}{7}$ $\frac{10}{7\frac{1}{2}}$ $\frac{10}{8}$ $\frac{10\frac{3}{4}}{8\frac{1}{2}}$ $\frac{10\frac{3}{4}}{9}$ $\frac{11\frac{1}{2}}{9\frac{1}{2}}$ $\frac{}{10}$ in.

#### STEAMER BOTTOMS.

$\frac{9\frac{1}{2}}{6}$ $\frac{9\frac{3}{4}}{6\frac{1}{2}}$ $\frac{9\frac{3}{4}}{7}$ $\frac{10\frac{1}{2}}{7\frac{1}{2}}$ $\frac{10\frac{1}{2}}{8}$ $\frac{11\frac{1}{2}}{8\frac{1}{2}}$ $\frac{11\frac{1}{2}}{9}$ $\frac{}{9\frac{1}{2}}$ in.

#### BOSTON & MAINE FOUNDRY COMPANY.

Pots. $\frac{9\frac{1}{2}}{6}$, $\frac{10\frac{1}{2}}{7}$ $\frac{11\frac{1}{2}}{8}$ $\frac{13}{9}$ in.  Kettles. $\frac{8\frac{3}{4}}{6}$ $\frac{9\frac{1}{2}}{7}$ $\frac{10\frac{1}{2}}{8}$ $\frac{11\frac{1}{4}}{9}$ in.

#### BARSTOW.

Pots. $\frac{9\frac{1}{4}}{6}$ $\frac{10\frac{1}{4}}{7}$ $\frac{11\frac{1}{4}}{8}$ $\frac{12\frac{1}{2}}{9}$ in.  Kettles. $\frac{9}{6}$ $\frac{9\frac{3}{4}}{7}$ $\frac{10\frac{1}{2}}{8}$ $\frac{11\frac{1}{4}}{9}$ in.

#### NEW MARKET.

Pots. $\frac{9\frac{3}{4}}{6}$ $\frac{10\frac{1}{2}}{7}$ $\frac{11\frac{1}{2}}{8}$ $\frac{12\frac{1}{2}}{9}$ in.  Kettles. $\frac{9\frac{1}{4}}{6}$ $\frac{9\frac{3}{4}}{7}$ $\frac{10\frac{1}{4}}{8}$ $\frac{11\frac{1}{4}}{9}$ in.

#### GOEWAY'S COMMON.

Pots. $\frac{8}{6}$ $\frac{9}{7}$ $\frac{10\frac{1}{4}}{8}$ $\frac{11\frac{1}{4}}{9}$ in.  Kettles. $\frac{8\frac{1}{4}}{6}$ $\frac{9\frac{1}{4}}{7}$ $\frac{10}{8}$ $\frac{10\frac{1}{2}}{9}$ in.

#### GOEWAY'S EXTRA.

Pots. $\frac{9}{6}$ $\frac{10\frac{1}{4}}{7}$ $\frac{11\frac{1}{4}}{8}$ $\frac{11\frac{1}{2}}{9}$ in.  Kettles. $\frac{8\frac{1}{2}}{6}$ $\frac{9\frac{3}{4}}{7}$ $\frac{10\frac{1}{2}}{8}$ $\frac{11}{9}$ in.

#### RICHARDSON'S.

Pots. $\frac{10}{6}$ $\frac{10\frac{3}{4}}{7}$ $\frac{11\frac{3}{4}}{8}$ $\frac{13}{9}$ in.  Kettles. $\frac{9\frac{3}{4}}{6}$ $\frac{10\frac{1}{2}}{7}$ $\frac{11\frac{1}{4}}{8}$ $\frac{13}{9}$ in.

#### PALMER & CO.

Pots. $\frac{8\frac{1}{2}}{6}$ $\frac{9}{7}$ $\frac{10\frac{1}{4}}{8}$ $\frac{11\frac{1}{4}}{9}$ $\frac{11\frac{1}{2}}{10}$ in.  Kettles. $\frac{8\frac{1}{2}}{6}$ $\frac{8\frac{3}{4}}{7}$ $\frac{9\frac{3}{4}}{8}$ $\frac{10\frac{1}{2}}{9}$ $\frac{12\frac{1}{2}}{10}$ in.

#### RATHBURN & CO.

Pots. $\frac{8\frac{3}{4}}{7}$ $\frac{9\frac{3}{4}}{8}$ $\frac{10\frac{1}{2}}{9}$ $\frac{11\frac{3}{4}}{10}$ in.  Kettles. $\frac{9}{7}$ $\frac{9\frac{3}{4}}{8}$ $\frac{10\frac{1}{2}}{9}$ $\frac{11\frac{1}{4}}{10}$ in.

## STOVE HOLLOW WARE.

### POTS.

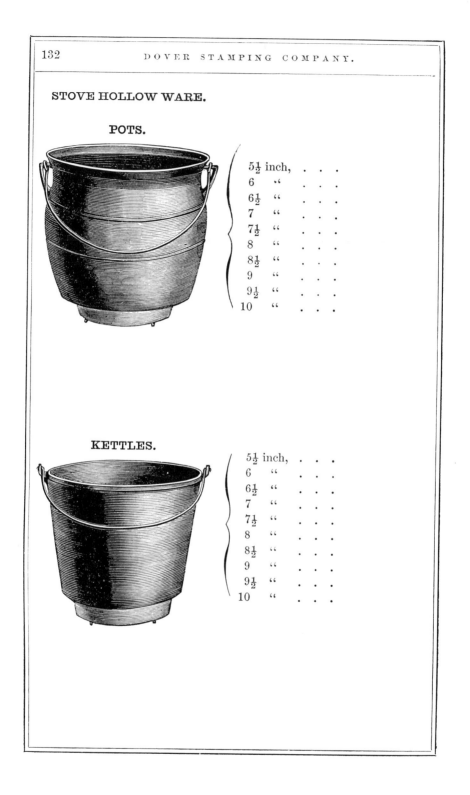

| | |
|---|---|
| $5\frac{1}{2}$ inch, | . . . |
| 6 " | . . . |
| $6\frac{1}{2}$ " | . . . |
| 7 " | . . . |
| $7\frac{1}{2}$ " | . . . |
| 8 " | . . . |
| $8\frac{1}{2}$ " | . . . |
| 9 " | . . . |
| $9\frac{1}{2}$ " | . . . |
| 10 " | . . . |

### KETTLES.

| | |
|---|---|
| $5\frac{1}{2}$ inch, | . . . |
| 6 " | . . . |
| $6\frac{1}{2}$ " | . . . |
| 7 " | . . . |
| $7\frac{1}{2}$ " | . . . |
| 8 " | . . . |
| $8\frac{1}{2}$ " | . . . |
| 9 " | . . . |
| $9\frac{1}{2}$ " | . . . |
| 10 " | . . . |

## STOVE HOLLOW WARE.

### TEA KETTLES.

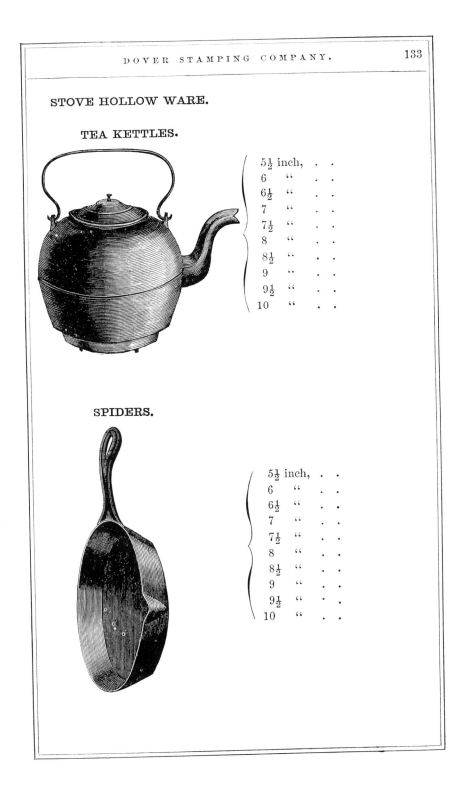

5½ inch, . .
6 " . .
6½ " . .
7 " . .
7½ " . .
8 " . .
8½ " . .
9 " . .
9½ " . .
10 " . .

### SPIDERS.

5½ inch, . .
6 " . .
6½ " . .
7 " . .
7½ " . .
8 " . .
8½ " . .
9 " . .
9½ " . .
10 " . .

## STOVE
## HOLLOW WARE.

**TEA KETTLES.**

SLIDE OR SWING COVERS.

$\left\{ \begin{array}{l} \text{6 inch,} \quad . \quad . \quad . \quad . \\ \text{7 “} \quad\quad . \quad . \quad . \quad . \\ \text{8 “} \quad\quad . \quad . \quad . \quad . \\ \text{9 “} \quad\quad . \quad . \quad . \quad . \\ \text{10 ”} \quad\quad . \quad . \quad . \quad . \end{array} \right.$

**IN SETS.**

POT, KETTLE,
TEA KETTLE and SPIDER.

$\left\{ \begin{array}{l} 5\tfrac{1}{2} \text{ inch,} \quad . \quad . \quad . \\ \text{6 “} \quad\quad . \quad . \quad . \\ 6\tfrac{1}{2} \text{ “} \quad\quad . \quad . \quad . \\ \text{7 “} \quad\quad . \quad . \quad . \\ 7\tfrac{1}{2} \text{ “} \quad\quad . \quad . \quad . \\ \text{8 “} \quad\quad . \quad . \quad . \\ 8\tfrac{1}{2} \text{ “} \quad\quad . \quad . \quad . \\ \text{9 “} \quad\quad . \quad . \quad . \\ 9\tfrac{1}{2} \text{ ”} \quad\quad . \quad . \quad . \\ \text{10 “} \quad\quad . \quad . \quad . \end{array} \right.$

The *Tops* of the sizes expressed by the " $\tfrac{1}{2}$ inch" correspond to the size larger ware, thus — an $8\tfrac{1}{2}$ inch has an 8 inch sink and 9 inch top.

Our Hollow Ware is made with the utmost care, light and smooth, and is sold by the piece or in sets, with or without **Tea** Kettle.

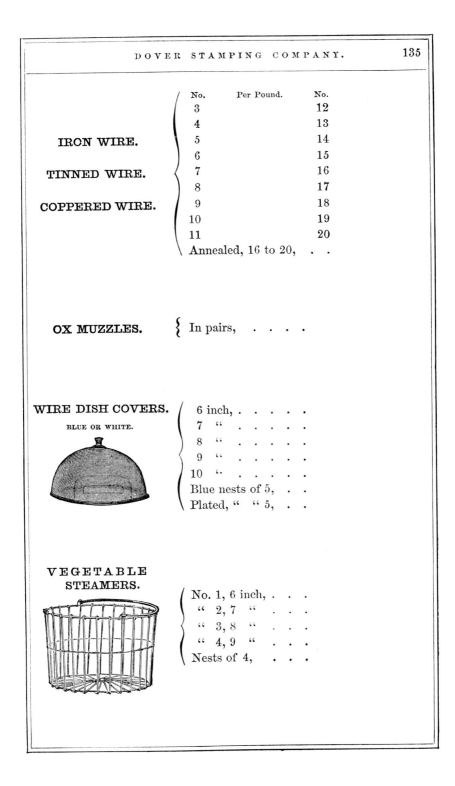

|  | No. | Per Pound. | No. |
|---|---|---|---|
|  | 3 |  | 12 |
|  | 4 |  | 13 |
| **IRON WIRE.** | 5 |  | 14 |
|  | 6 |  | 15 |
| **TINNED WIRE.** | 7 |  | 16 |
|  | 8 |  | 17 |
| **COPPERED WIRE.** | 9 |  | 18 |
|  | 10 |  | 19 |
|  | 11 |  | 20 |
|  | Annealed, 16 to 20, | . . |  |

**OX MUZZLES.** In pairs, . . . .

**WIRE DISH COVERS.**

BLUE OR WHITE.

6 inch, . . . . .
7 " . . . . .
8 " . . . . .
9 " . . . . .
10 " . . . . .
Blue nests of 5, . .
Plated, " " 5, . .

**VEGETABLE STEAMERS.**

No. 1, 6 inch, . . .
" 2, 7 " . . .
" 3, 8 " . . .
" 4, 9 " . . .
Nests of 4, . . .

## PATENT
## TENON BROILERS.

TINNED.

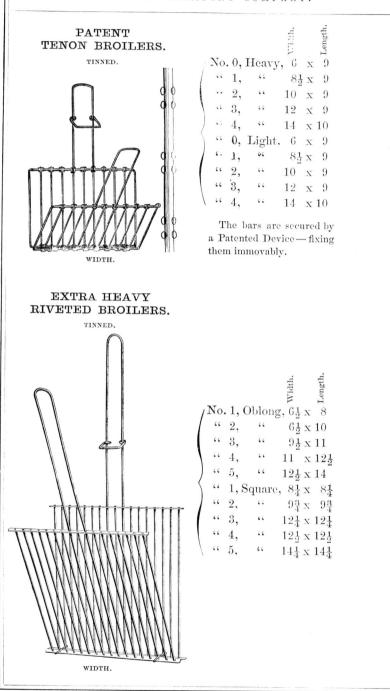

WIDTH.

| | Width. | | Length. |
|---|---|---|---|
| No. 0, Heavy, | 6 | x | 9 |
| " 1, " | 8½ | x | 9 |
| " 2, " | 10 | x | 9 |
| " 3, " | 12 | x | 9 |
| " 4, " | 14 | x | 10 |
| " 0, Light. | 6 | x | 9 |
| " 1, " | 8½ | x | 9 |
| " 2, " | 10 | x | 9 |
| " 3, " | 12 | x | 9 |
| " 4, " | 14 | x | 10 |

The bars are secured by
a Patented Device—fixing
them immovably.

## EXTRA HEAVY
## RIVETED BROILERS.

TINNED.

WIDTH.

| | Width. | | Length. |
|---|---|---|---|
| No. 1, Oblong, | 6½ | x | 8 |
| " 2, " | 6½ | x | 10 |
| " 3, " | 9½ | x | 11 |
| " 4, " | 11 | x | 12½ |
| " 5, " | 12½ | x | 14 |
| " 1, Square, | 8¼ | x | 8¼ |
| " 2, " | 9¾ | x | 9¾ |
| " 3, " | 12¼ | x | 12¼ |
| " 4, " | 12½ | x | 12½ |
| " 5, " | 14¼ | x | 14¼ |

## PATENT BROILERS OR TOASTERS.

LIGHT, CORRUGATED.

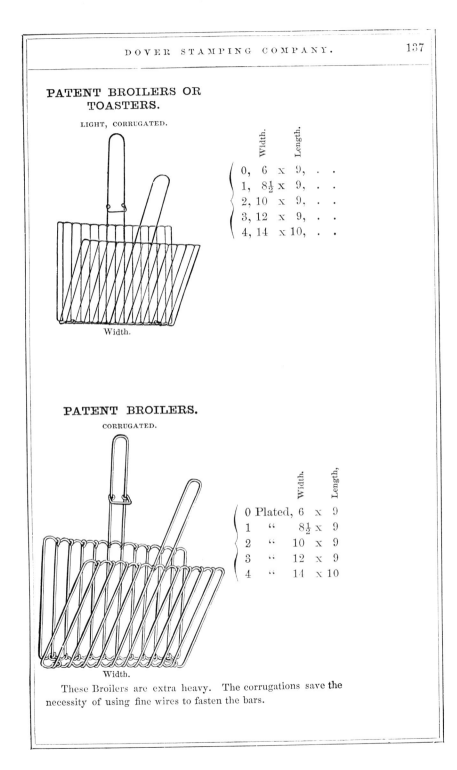

Width.

| | | Width. | | Length. |
|---|---|---|---|---|
| 0, | 6 | x | 9, | . . |
| 1, | 8½ | x | 9, | . . |
| 2, | 10 | x | 9, | . . |
| 3, | 12 | x | 9, | . . |
| 4, | 14 | x | 10, | . . |

## PATENT BROILERS.

CORRUGATED.

| | | | Width. | | Length, |
|---|---|---|---|---|---|
| 0 Plated, | | 6 | x | 9 | |
| 1 | " | 8½ | x | 9 | |
| 2 | " | 10 | x | 9 | |
| 3 | " | 12 | x | 9 | |
| 4 | " | 14 | x | 10 | |

Width.

These Broilers are extra heavy. The corrugations save the necessity of using fine wires to fasten the bars.

## CORN POPPERS.

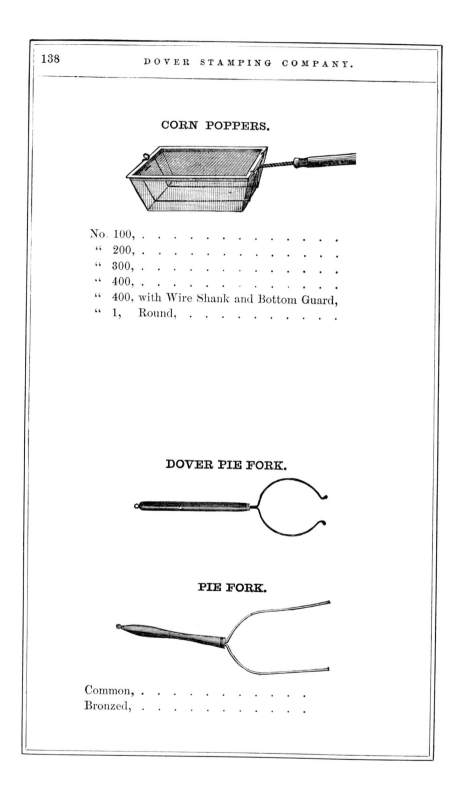

No. 100, . . . . . . . . . .
" 200, . . . . . . . . . .
" 300, . . . . . . . . . .
" 400, . . . . . . . . . .
" 400, with Wire Shank and Bottom Guard,
" 1,    Round, . . . . . . . . .

## DOVER PIE FORK.

## PIE FORK.

Common, . . . . . . . . .
Bronzed, . . . . . . . . .

**PEA SKIMMERS.**

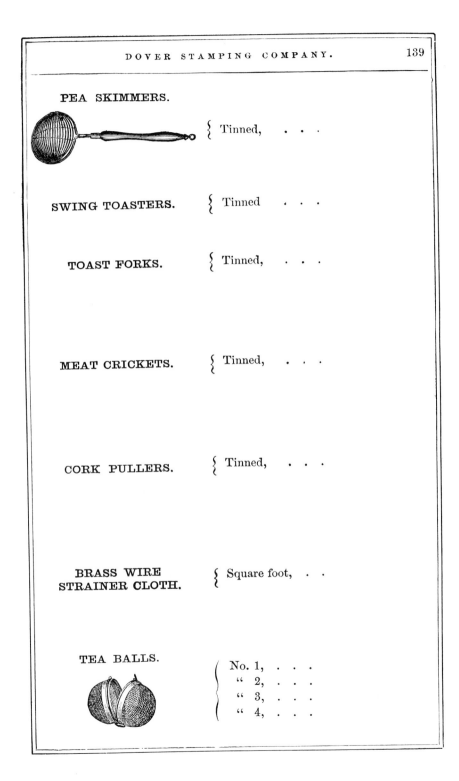

{ Tinned, . . .

**SWING TOASTERS.** { Tinned . . .

**TOAST FORKS.** { Tinned, . . .

**MEAT CRICKETS.** { Tinned, . . .

**CORK PULLERS.** { Tinned, . . .

**BRASS WIRE STRAINER CLOTH.** { Square foot, . .

**TEA BALLS.**

{ No. 1, . . .
  " 2, . . .
  " 3, . . .
  " 4, . . .

### EARLE'S PATENT EGG BEATER.

{ No. 1,   .   .   .   .   .

    This, while it is the simplest, is the most effective Egg Beater made. Held in the hand with an immovable rest, it stands firmly wherever placed and will beat eggs with greater rapidity than any other ; while the price places it within the reach of all. It is cleaned by a moment's rapid turning in hot water.

### MUNROE'S PATENT. EGG BEATER.

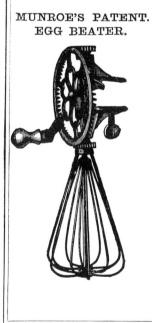

{ Family size,   .   .   .
Mammoth, for Hotels
   and Bakeries,   .   .

    This Beater is too well known to the public to need our commendation

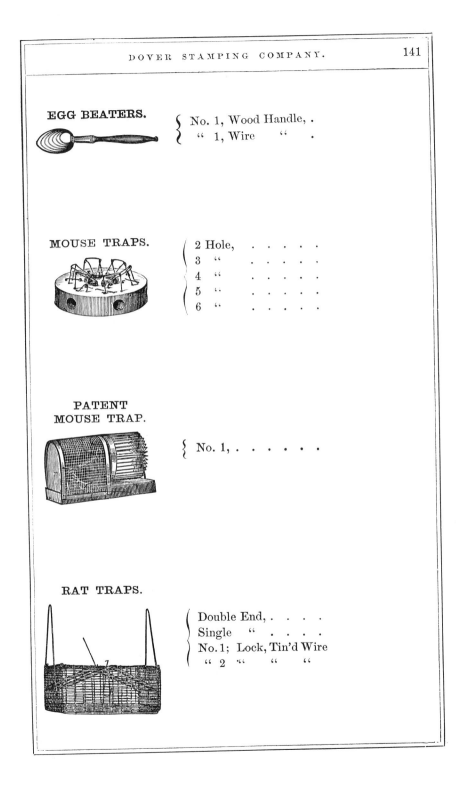

**EGG BEATERS.**

No. 1, Wood Handle, .

" 1, Wire    "    .

**MOUSE TRAPS.**

2 Hole, . . . . .

3 " . . . . .

4 " . . . . .

5 " . . . . .

6 " . . . . .

**PATENT
MOUSE TRAP.**

No. 1, . . . . . .

**RAT TRAPS.**

Double End, . . . .

Single " . . . .

No. 1; Lock, Tin'd Wire

" 2 " " "

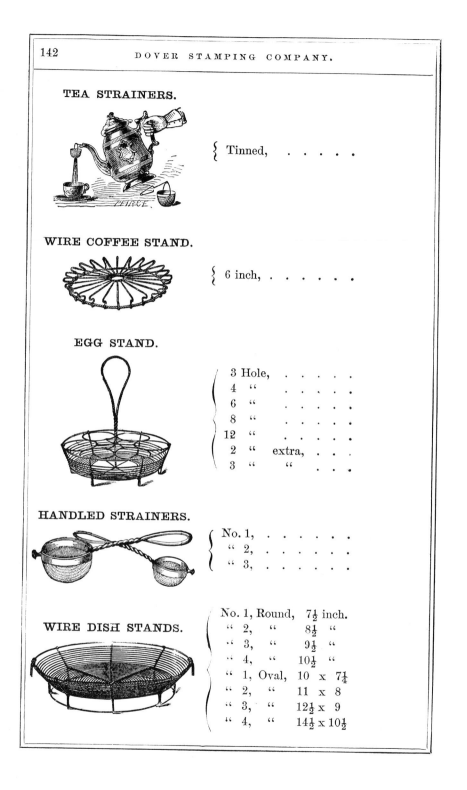

## TEA STRAINERS.

{ Tinned, . . . . .

## WIRE COFFEE STAND.

{ 6 inch, . . . . . .

## EGG STAND.

{
3 Hole, . . . . .
4 " . . . .
6 " . . . .
8 " . . . .
12 " . . . .
2 " extra, . . .
3 " " . . .

## HANDLED STRAINERS.

{
No. 1, . . . . . .
" 2, . . . . . .
" 3, . . . . . .

## WIRE DISH STANDS.

{
No. 1, Round, 7½ inch.
" 2, " 8½ "
" 3, " 9½ "
" 4, " 10½ "
" 1, Oval, 10 x 7¼
" 2, " 11 x 8
" 3, " 12½ x 9
" 4, " 14½ x 10½

## BREAKFAST CASTER.

Holes. Bottles.
{ 3, No. 1, Brit. Top.
4, " 1, " "
3, " 2, Silver "
4, " 2, " "

## STANDARD CASTER.

Holes. Bottles.
{ 3, No. 11, Brit. Top.
3, " 12, Silver "
4, " 13, " "
4, " 14, " "

## WIRE FRUIT BASKET.

{ 9 inch Bowl, . . . .

## WIRE SIEVES.

### NESTS OF 3.

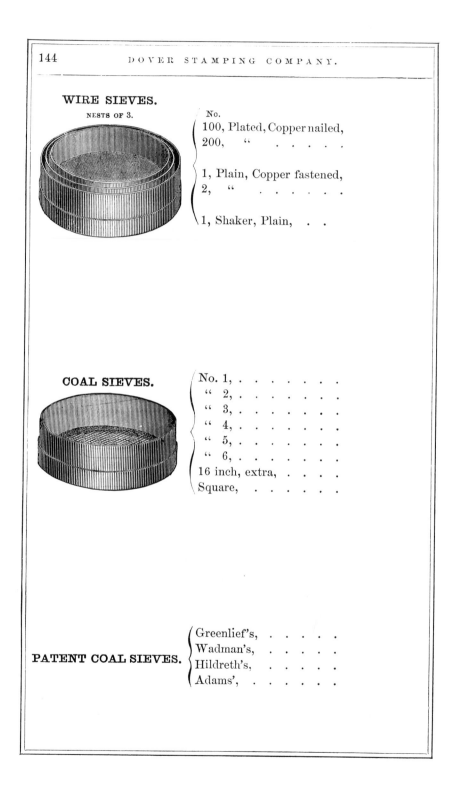

No.
100, Plated, Copper nailed,
200,　　"　　.　.　.　.　.

1, Plain, Copper fastened,
2,　　"　　.　.　.　.　.　.

1, Shaker, Plain,　.　.

## COAL SIEVES.

No. 1,　.　.　.　.　.　.
"　2,　.　.　.　.　.　.
"　3,　.　.　.　.　.　.
"　4,　.　.　.　.　.　.
"　5,　.　.　.　.　.　.
"　6,　.　.　.　.　.　.
16 inch, extra,　.　.　.　.
Square,　.　.　.　.　.　.

## PATENT COAL SIEVES.

Greenlief's,　.　.　.　.　.
Wadman's,　.　.　.　.　.
Hildreth's,　.　.　.　.　.
Adams',　.　.　.　.　.

## BLOOD'S PATENT COAL SIFTER.

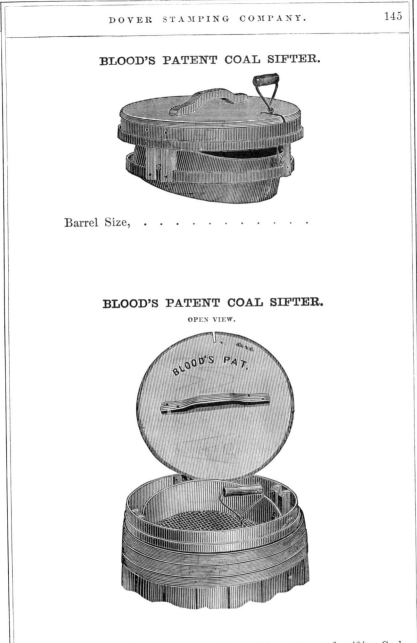

Barrel Size, . . . . . . . . . .

## BLOOD'S PATENT COAL SIFTER.

### OPEN VIEW.

Blood's Patent Coal Sieve, combines all the qualities necessary for sifting Coals. Compact, Durable, Cheap, and by far the most rapid ever yet made. The dust does not escape to soil the clothing. Is warranted to give perfect satisfaction.

# BLOOD'S PATENT SIFTERS.

Family Size, . . . . . . . . . .
Grocers' Size, . . . . . . . . .
Large, . . . . . . . . . . .

The wide-spread popularity of BLOOD'S PATENT SIFTER, the immense and increasing demand that has attended its introduction throughout the United States, its approval by every one who has aught to do in the kitchen, its rapid execution of whatever is required, its perfect adaptability to every kind of sifting or straining,— warrants us in saying that it has no equal or the semblance of one.

## THE PIONEER OF SIFTERS.

It holds the front rank. ITS VARIED AND PERFECT WORK entitles it to this position.

It sifts Flour and Corn Meal very much faster than any other, and with *perfect cleanliness.* Nor will it grind up insects or other foreign substances with the Flour.

AND YET ITS GREATEST SUPERIORITY IS NOT AS A FLOUR SIFTER.

In preparing Squash, Apple or Pumpkin for Pies, or other Fruits for Jams or Jellies, its value is increased a hundred fold.

These articles reduced to a consistency suitable for pies, are sent through at the rate of FOUR QUARTS in as many minutes.

### STEWED TOMATOES, CURRANTS, GRAPES, &c.,

leave their SEEDS and SKINS in the Sifter, while the PULP and JUICES are sent through with astonishing rapidity.

MOLASSES is seldom clean enough for use,—BLOOD'S SIFTER CLEANSES IT THOROUGHLY.

In the West it is used to strain SORGHUM as it comes from the Mill.

Those who do much with CREAM TARTAR find it invaluable. Druggists find it indispensable in

### SIFTING AND STRAINING THEIR VARIOUS MEDICINES.

So with Glaziers, in sifting WHITING. All this varied labor is performed by one of

## BLOOD'S SIFTERS,

While with a touch the inside is removed, and IT IS CLEANED AS EASILY AS WASHING A PLATE. Nor do the Acids affect in the least any part of the Sifter. The heavy TIN PLATING upon the Wire Cloth resists all action of Acids.

BLOOD'S PATENT COVERS THE

# VIBRATING ROLLERS,

### Imitators not daring to use these indispensable Rollers,

Or VIBRATING MOTION, have substituted various contrivances in hopes to answer the purpose. Among these are Cranks, India Rubber, Bristles, Leather, Stationary Wood, &c., &c. The objections to each and all of these are insuperable.

The Rubber, Bristles and Leather *impart their own odor* to whatever is sifted, to an extent sufficient to make it apparent in Bread, Pies, Jellies, &c.
Bristles collect and retain whatever is sifted, which sours and is filthy.

Stationary Wood scraping upon the wire gauze, wears it out in a few weeks, and also grinds fine whatever may be in the flour, whether insects or other substances.

Rubber and Bristles crumble and become incorporated with the bread or pies, constituting a violent poison.

None of these Imitations pretend to sift anything but Flour. They cannot even sift CORN MEAL, owing to the superabundance of bran.

Nor do any of them sift Flour so well or so rapidly as Blood's, by full one-half, while in sifting and straining fruits each and all are utter failures.

They avail themselves of the legitimate and increasing demand for

## Blood's Sifter, Strainer & Cullender

to force upon the unthinking public a sham, that after a few hours use is condemned, and turned over to its proper place, a plaything for children.

As SIFTER, STRAINER AND CULLENDER, all in one,—practicable, durable, cleanly, simple,—Blood's Patent claims the patronage of the public.

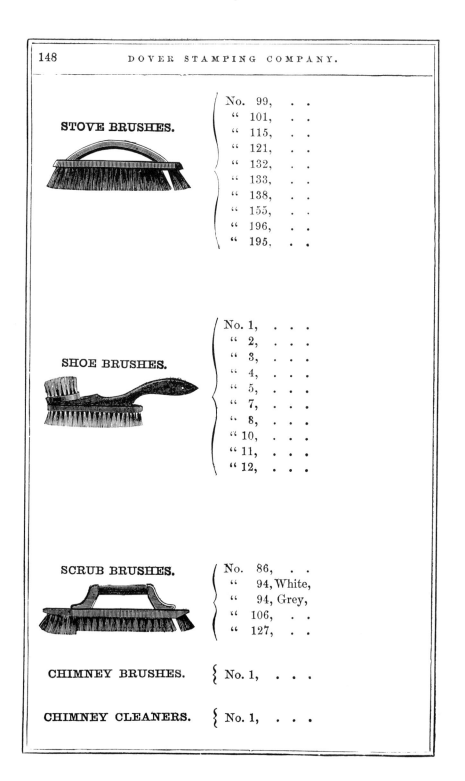

**STOVE BRUSHES.**

No. 99, . .
" 101, . .
" 115, . .
" 121, . .
" 132, . .
" 133, . .
" 138, . .
" 155, . .
" 196, . .
" 195, . .

**SHOE BRUSHES.**

No. 1, . . .
" 2, . . .
" 3, . . .
" 4, . . .
" 5, . . .
" 7, . . .
" 8, . . .
" 10, . . .
" 11, . . .
" 12, . . .

**SCRUB BRUSHES.**

No. 86, . .
" 94, White,
" 94, Grey,
" 106, . .
" 127, . .

**CHIMNEY BRUSHES.**   No. 1, . . .

**CHIMNEY CLEANERS.**   No. 1, . . .

## FLOOR BRUSHES.

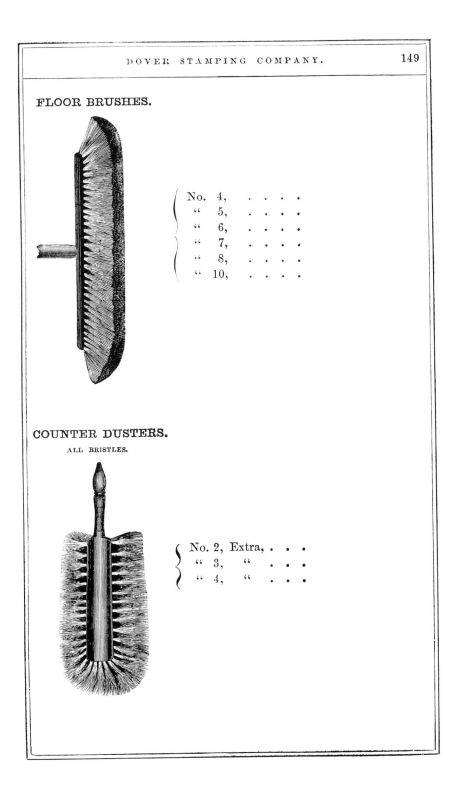

No. 4, . . . .
" 5, . . . .
" 6, . . . .
" 7, . . . .
" 8, . . . .
" 10, . . . .

## COUNTER DUSTERS.

ALL BRISTLES.

No. 2, Extra, . . .
" 3, " . . .
" 4, " . . .

## FOUNDRY GOODS.

**RIDDLES.**

$$
\left\{
\begin{array}{l}
\text{16 inch, Brass, 3 to 20, .} \\
\text{18 " " 3 to 20, .} \\
\text{20 " " 3 to 20, .} \\
\\
\text{16 inch, Iron, 3 to 20, .} \\
\text{18 " " 3 to 20, .} \\
\text{20 " " 3 to 20, .}
\end{array}
\right.
$$

Mesh.

**RIDDLES.**
HAND MADE, 13 x 14 WIRE.

$$
\left\{
\begin{array}{l}
\text{20 inch, Iron, 3 mesh, . .} \\
\text{22 " " 3 " . .}
\end{array}
\right.
$$

**SAND SCREENS.**
FROM $\frac{1}{8}$ TO $1\frac{2}{8}$ in. MESH.

$$\left\{ \text{6 feet x } 2\frac{3}{4} \text{ feet, . . .} \right.$$

**FOUNDRY SHOVELS.**

$$
\left\{
\begin{array}{l}
\text{1st quality, . . . . .} \\
\text{2nd " . . . . .}
\end{array}
\right.
$$

**CRUCIBLES.**

$$
\left\{
\begin{array}{l}
\text{Brass, . . . . . .} \\
\text{Steel, . . . . . .}
\end{array}
\right.
$$

**FOUNDRY DUSTERS.**

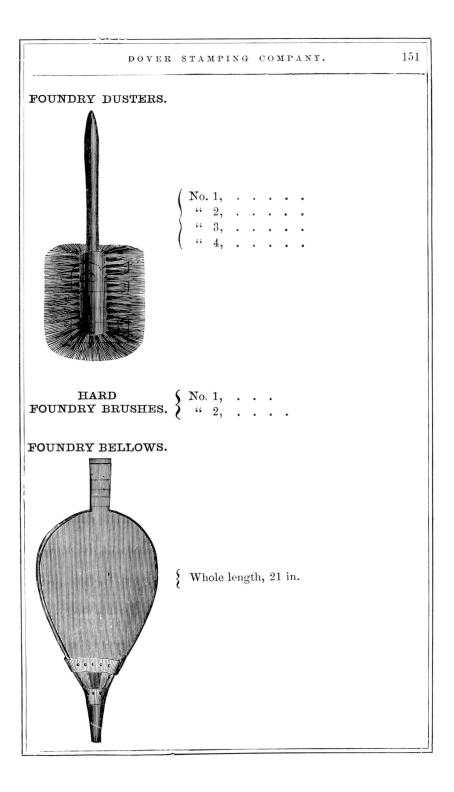

No. 1, . . . . .
" 2, . . . . .
" 3, . . . . .
" 4, . . . . .

**HARD**
**FOUNDRY BRUSHES.**  No. 1, . . .
" 2, . . . .

**FOUNDRY BELLOWS.**

Whole length, 21 in.

FOUNDRY GOODS.

**MOULDING TROWELS.**

{ No. 1, 5¼ in. Blade, . .
  " 2, 6½ " " .

**SQUARE TROWELS.**

{ 4¼ in. Blade, . . .

**STOVE MOULDERS' TROWELS.**

{ No. 1, 4¾ in. Blade, .
  " 2, 5¼ " " . .
  " 3, 6 " " . .

**STRAIGHT SLICKERS.**

ROUND LIFT.

{ No. 1, 8 in. Long, .
  " 2, 10 " " . ,
  " 3, 12 " " . .

**STRAIGHT SLICKERS.**

SQUARE LIFT.

{ No. 1, 8 in. Long, .
  " 2, 10 " " . .
  " 3, 12 " " . .

**CROOKED SLICKERS.**

SQUARE LIFT.

| | Length. |
|---|---|
| No. 1, | 8 in. . . |
| " 2, | 10 " . . |
| " 3, | 12 " . . |
| " 1, Brass, | 8 " . . |
| " 2, " | 10 " . . |

These goods are of the very best Spring-tempered Steel — perfectly true — and polished as highly as they *can* be. They are warranted superior to any in use.

## FOUNDRY FACINGS.

SEA COAL, { For Light Castings, . . . . <br> { " Heavy " . .

LEHIGH, . . . . . . . . . . . . . . . .

CHARCOAL, . . . . . . . . . . . . .

CLARK'S, . . . . . . . . . . . . . .

LEAD, . . . . . . . . . . . . . . .

PLUMBAGO, { Extra fine, . . . . . .

SOAPSTONE, { No. 2, . . . . . . . <br> { " 1, Extra Bolted, .

SOCANNOSSET, . . . . . . . . . . . .

PLATE FACING, . . . . . . . . . . .

We take special pains to produce the VERY BEST article of Facings.

## STOVE POLISH.

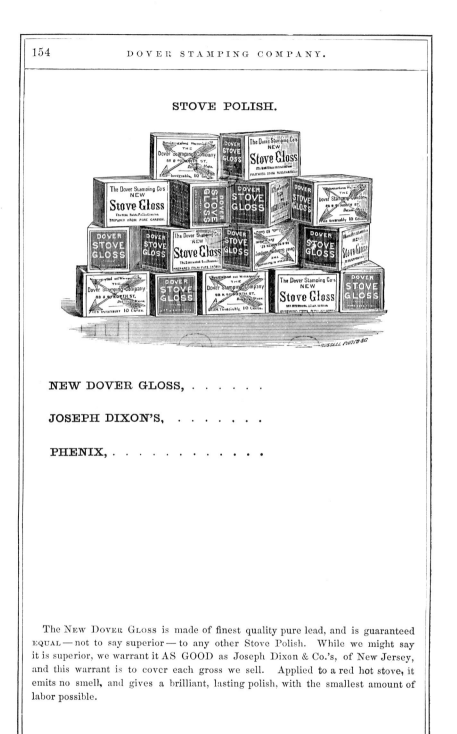

NEW DOVER GLOSS, . . . . . .

JOSEPH DIXON'S, . . . . . . .

PHENIX, . . . . . . . . . . .

The NEW DOVER GLOSS is made of finest quality pure lead, and is guaranteed EQUAL — not to say superior — to any other Stove Polish. While we might say it is superior, we warrant it AS GOOD as Joseph Dixon & Co.'s, of New Jersey, and this warrant is to cover each gross we sell. Applied to a red hot stove, it emits no smell, and gives a brilliant, lasting polish, with the smallest amount of labor possible.

## BLACK LEAD IN BULK.

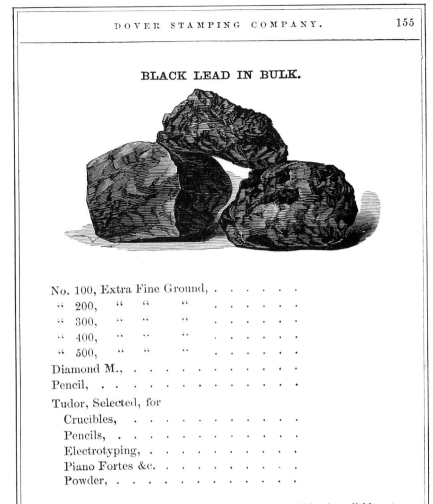

No. 100, Extra Fine Ground, . . . . . . .
" 200, " " " . . . . . .
" 300, " " " . . . . . .
" 400, " " " . . . . . .
" 500, " " " . . . . . .
Diamond M., . . . . . . . . . .
Pencil, . . . . . . . . . . .
Tudor, Selected, for
  Crucibles, . . . . . . . . . .
  Pencils, . . . . . . . . . .
  Electrotyping, . . . . . . . . .
  Piano Fortes &c. . . . . . . . .
  Powder, . . . . . . . . . . .

The above grades Black Lead embrace the different qualities for polishing stoves or for manufacturing into Stove Polish. The numbers from 100 to 500 inclusive are taken from the celebrated Tudor Mine, unusually rich in carbon, and producing a deep lustre.

The clear Tudor Lead, selected, is celebrated for the extra fine quality ERASIVE PENCILS made from it by all the New England Pencil makers; also for its powers of resistance to heat which adapts it to the production of Crucibles.

It is warranted superior to any in this country, and fully equal to the best in Europe.

Our stock embraces at all times the largest variety of Black Lead in the country crude or prepared for Stove Polish, Pencils, Crucibles, Electrotyping, Piano Fortes, Lubricating Machinery and all other purposes for which the article is used.

## METALS.

**WIRE.**
{ From     4 to 20,   .
Annealed 16 to 20,   .

**SHEET COPPER.**
14 Oz,,   .   .   .   .
16   "     .   .   .   .
18   "     .   .   .   .
Tinning extra,   .   .   .

**COPPER BOTTOMS.** { All kinds.   .   .   .   .

**SOLDER.**
{ No. 1,   .   .   .   .
" 2,   .   .   .   .

**PLIERS.**

in.
$4\frac{1}{2}$ Flat Nose,   .   .   .
5   "   "   .   .   .
$5\frac{1}{2}$ "   "   .   .   .
6   "   "   .   .   .
$6\frac{1}{2}$ "   "   .   .   .
7   "   "   .   .   .
8   "   "   .   .   .
9   "   "   .   .   .

$4\frac{1}{2}$ Round Nose,   .   .
5   "   "   .   .
$5\frac{1}{2}$ "   "   .   .
6   "   "   .   .
$6\frac{1}{2}$ "   "   .   .
7   "   "   .   .
8   "   "   .   .
9   "   "   .   .

5   Straight Rd. Nose,
$5\frac{1}{2}$ "   "   "
6   "   "   "
$6\frac{1}{2}$ "   "   "

# TINNERS,

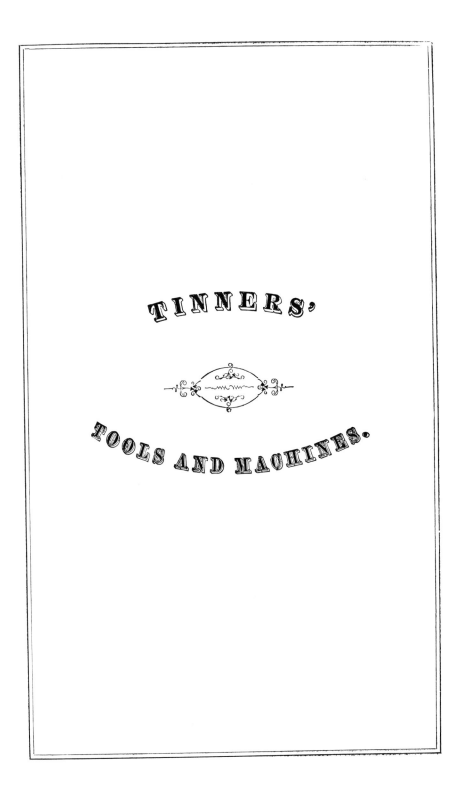

# TOOLS AND MACHINES.

**FILES.**

Inch.
10, Flat Bastard,   .
11,   "    "     .
12,   "    "     .
13,   "    "     .
14,   "    "     .
10, Half Round,  .  .
11,   "    "     .  .
12,   "    "     .  .
13,   "    "     .  .
14,   "    "     .  .

**HORSE RASPS.**

12 inch,   .  .  .  .
13   "    .  .  .  .

**TAPER FILES.**

4 inch,   .  .  .  .
4½ "    .  .  .  .
5 "    .  .  .  .
5½ "    .  .  .  .
6 "    .  .  .  .

**STEEL SQUARES.**

No. 3, 24 inch,   .  .
" 10, 12  "     .  .

**IRON SQUARES.**

No. 2, 24 inch,   .  .

## C. S. DIVIDERS.

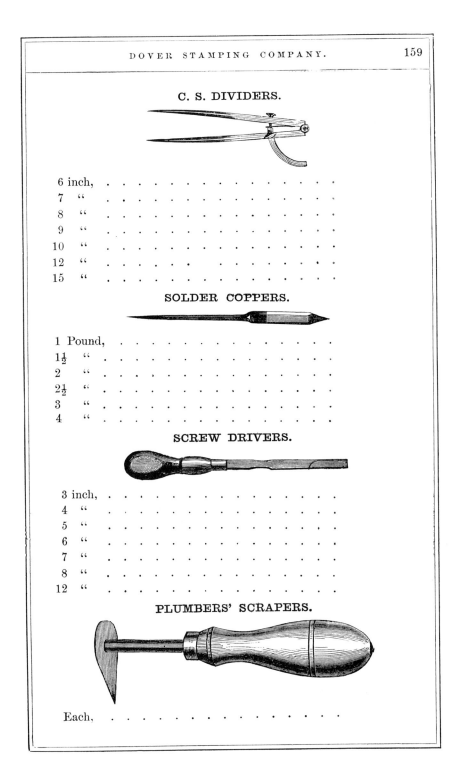

6 inch, . . . . . . . . . . . .
7  " . . . . . . . . . . . .
8  " . . . . . . . . . . . .
9  " . . . . . . . . . . . .
10  " . . . . . . . . . . . .
12  " . . . . . . . . . . . .
15  " . . . . . . . . . . . .

## SOLDER COPPERS.

1 Pound, . . . . . . . . . . .
1½  " . . . . . . . . . . .
2  " . . . . . . . . . . .
2½  " . . . . . . . . . . .
3  " . . . . . . . . . . .
4  " . . . . . . . . . . .

## SCREW DRIVERS.

3 inch, . . . . . . . . . . .
4  " . . . . . . . . . . .
5  " . . . . . . . . . . .
6  " . . . . . . . . . . .
7  " . . . . . . . . . . .
8  " . . . . . . . . . . .
12  " . . . . . . . . . . .

## PLUMBERS' SCRAPERS.

Each, . . . . . . . . . . . . .

**MALLETS.**

| | Length. | Diameter. |
|---|---|---|
| No. 5, | 5½ in. | 2 in. . |
| " 4. | 5½ " | 2½ " . |
| " 3, | 5½ " | 2¾ " . |
| " 2, | 6½ " | 3 " . |
| " 1, | 6¾ " | 3½ " . |
| " 0, | 7½ " | 4 " . |

**SOLDER COPPER HANDLES.**  { One size, . . . .

**SCRATCH AWLS.**  { No. 1, . . . . .
                     " 2, . . . . .

**WIRE GAUGES.**  { Small, Round, . .
                    Large, " . . .
                    Oblong, . . . .

**SLATE PENCILS.**  { 4 Inch, . . . . .
                      6 " . . . . .

## GEARED DRILLS.

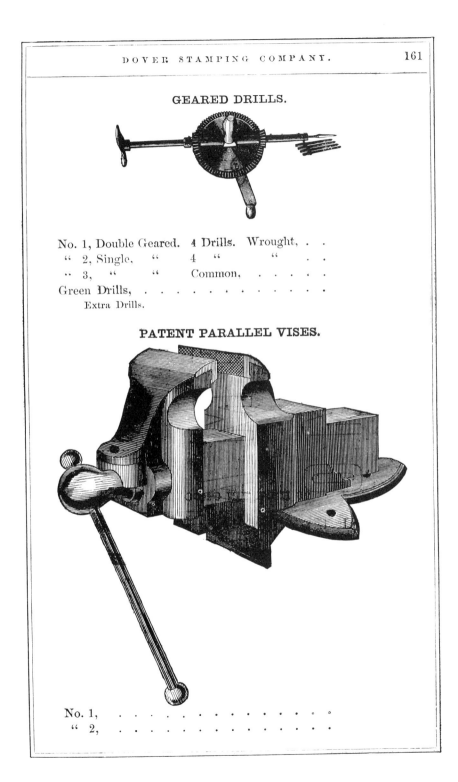

No. 1, Double Geared. 4 Drills. Wrought, . .
" 2, Single, " 4 " " . .
.. 3, " " Common, . . . . .
Green Drills, . . . . . . . . . .
    Extra Drills.

## PATENT PARALLEL VISES.

No. 1, . . . . . . . . . . . .
" 2, . . . . . . . . . . . .

# WHITNEY'S
# TOOLS AND MACHINES.

### 20 INCH TIN FOLDER.

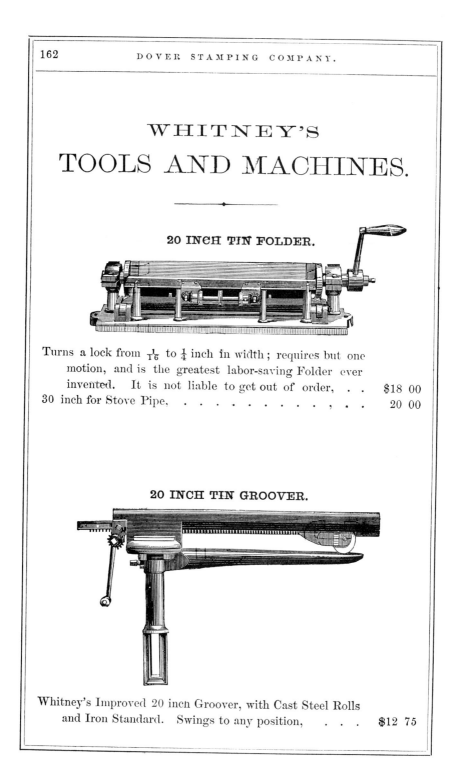

Turns a lock from $\frac{1}{16}$ to $\frac{1}{4}$ inch in width; requires but one motion, and is the greatest labor-saving Folder ever invented.   It is not liable to get out of order, . .   $18 00
30 inch for Stove Pipe, . . . . . . . . . . , . .   20 00

### 20 INCH TIN GROOVER.

Whitney's Improved 20 inch Groover, with Cast Steel Rolls and Iron Standard.   Swings to any position,   . . .   $12 75

## WIRING MACHINE.

Whitney's Patent Improved Wiring Machine, with Cast Steel Rolls, Rocking Box and Adjustable Collar, and Iron Standard that will fit any of the following machines in the set, . . . . $11 50

## SETTING-DOWN MACHINE.

Whitney's Patent Improved Setting Down Machine, with Cast Steel Rolls, Rocking Box, Adjustable Collar and Iron Standard, . $9 25

## SMALL TURNING MACHINE.

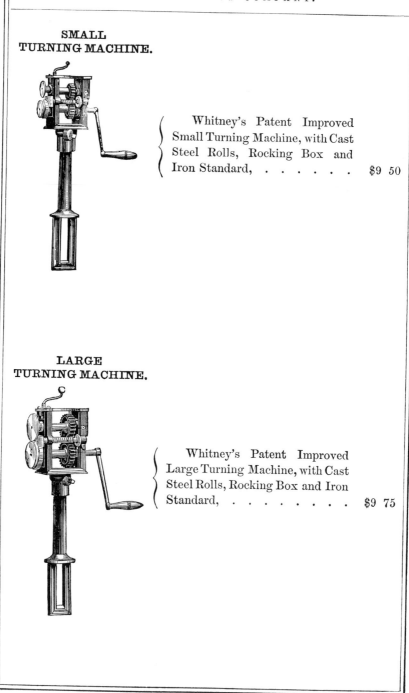

{ Whitney's Patent Improved Small Turning Machine, with Cast Steel Rolls, Rocking Box and Iron Standard, . . . . . . $9 50

## LARGE TURNING MACHINE.

{ Whitney's Patent Improved Large Turning Machine, with Cast Steel Rolls, Rocking Box and Iron Standard, . . . . . . . . $9 75

### SMALL
### BURRING MACHINE.

{ Whitney's Patent Improved Small Burring Machine, with Cast Steel Rolls, Rocking Box, Adjustable Collar and Iron Standard, . $8 00

### LARGE
### BURRING MACHINE.

{ Whitney's Patent Improved Large Burring Machine, with Cast Steel Rolls, Rocking Box, Adjustable Collar, and Iron Standard, . $8 50

It is conceded by those who have used Whitney's Machines that they are the best and cheapest in the world. Steel Rolls upon all. Will be warranted in every respect.

## FULL SET OF WHITNEY'S MACHINES.

Folding Machine, 20 in. . . . . . . . .

Grooving Machine, 20 in. . . . . . . . .

Wiring Machine and Stand, . . . . . . .

Large Turning Machine and Stand, . . . . . .

Small Turning Machine and Stand. . . . . . .

Large Burring Machine and Stand, . . . - . .

Small Burring Machine and Stand, . . . . . .

Setting Down Machine and Stand, . . . . . .

Full Set, with Stands, . . . . . . . .

WIRING STANDARD.

$1 00

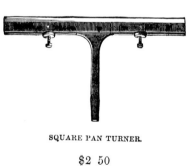

SQUARE PAN TURNER.

$2 50

## BEADING MACHINES.

COMMON NO. 2.                    NOS. 1, 3, & 4 IMPROVED.

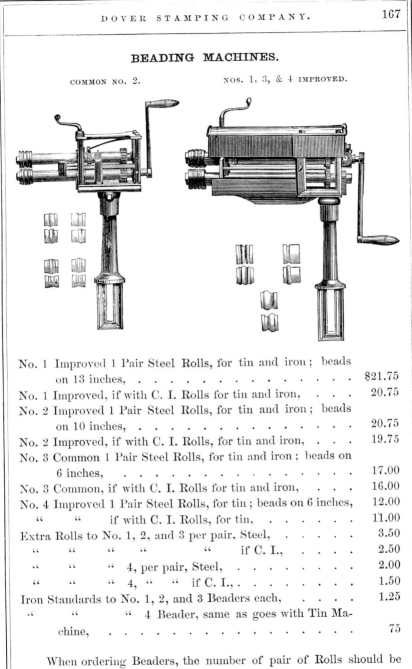

No. 1 Improved 1 Pair Steel Rolls, for tin and iron; beads
    on 13 inches, . . . . . . . . . . . . . . . $21.75

No. 1 Improved, if with C. I. Rolls for tin and iron, . . . 20.75

No. 2 Improved 1 Pair Steel Rolls, for tin and iron; beads
    on 10 inches, . . . . . . . . . . . . . . . 20.75

No. 2 Improved, if with C. I. Rolls, for tin and iron, . . . 19.75

No. 3 Common 1 Pair Steel Rolls, for tin and iron; beads on
    6 inches, . . . . . . . . . . . . . . . 17.00

No. 3 Common, if with C. I. Rolls for tin and iron, . . . 16.00

No. 4 Improved 1 Pair Steel Rolls, for tin; beads on 6 inches, 12.00

   "    "    if with C. I. Rolls, for tin, . . . . . . 11.00

Extra Rolls to No. 1, 2, and 3 per pair, Steel, . . . . . 3.50

  "   "   "   "     "   if C. I., . . . . 2.50

  "   "   " 4, per pair, Steel, . . . . . . . . 2.00

  "   "   " 4,  "   " if C. I., . . . . . . . . 1.50

Iron Standards to No. 1, 2, and 3 Beaders each, . . . . 1.25

  "    "     " 4 Beader, same as goes with Tin Machine, . . . . . . . . . . . . . . . . . . 75

    When ordering Beaders, the number of pair of Rolls should be
stated. Can furnish a great variety of Beads.

## TIN PIPE FORMER.

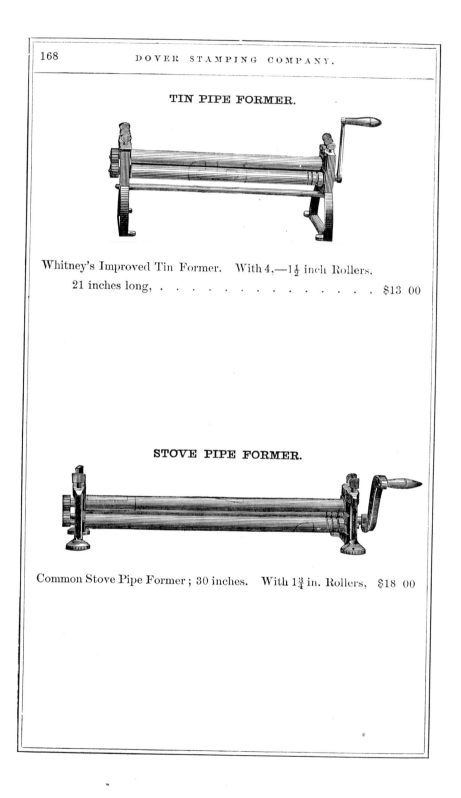

Whitney's Improved Tin Former.   With 4,—1½ inch Rollers.
21 inches long, . . . . . . . . . . . . . . . $13 00

## STOVE PIPE FORMER.

Common Stove Pipe Former ; 30 inches.   With 1¾ in. Rollers,   $18 00

## IMPROVED STOVE PIPE FORMER.

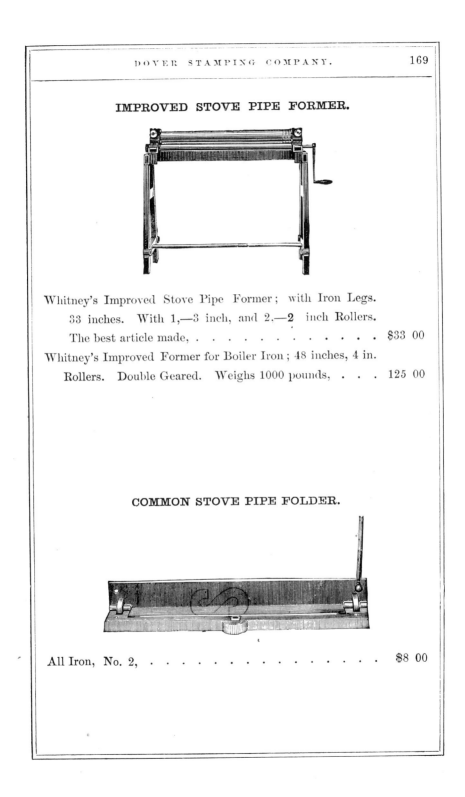

Whitney's Improved Stove Pipe Former; with Iron Legs.
  33 inches. With 1,—3 inch, and 2.—2 inch Rollers.
  The best article made, . . . . . . . . . . . . . $33 00
Whitney's Improved Former for Boiler Iron; 48 inches, 4 in.
  Rollers. Double Geared. Weighs 1000 pounds, . . . 125 00

## COMMON STOVE PIPE FOLDER.

All Iron, No. 2, . . . . . . . . . . . . . . . . $8 00

## GAUGE or SQUARING SHEARS.

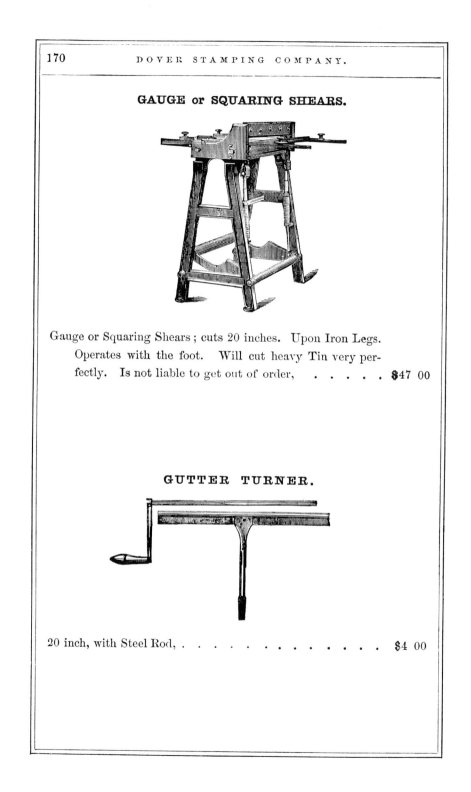

Gauge or Squaring Shears ; cuts 20 inches.  Upon Iron Legs.
Operates with the foot.   Will cut heavy Tin very perfectly.   Is not liable to get out of order,  .  .  .  .  . **$47** 00

## GUTTER TURNER.

20 inch, with Steel Rod, .  .  .  .  .  .  .  .  .  .  .  .  . **$4** 00

## SPAULDING'S PATENT TINNER'S PRESS.

Price, Net,                    $50.00.

# TINSMITHS CAN STAMP THEIR OWN COVERS!

Each Complete Machine will make the following size covers :

| Pail Covers. | | | Coffee Pot Covers. | | | |
|---|---|---|---|---|---|---|
| 1 Pint | | | 1 Quart | | | |
| 1 Quart | " | " | 2 " | " | " | " |
| 3 Pint or 2 Qt. | " | " | 3 " | " | " | " |
| 4 " | " | " | 4 " | " | " | " |
| 6 " | " | " | 5 " | " | " | " |
| 10 " | " | " | Wash Bowl Bottoms. | | | |

Any other size can be made by procuring EXTRA HEADS, which will be made to order. *A Boy 15 years of age,* with a *single hour's practice,* can make of either the above sizes Covers, from EIGHT TO TWELVE DOZEN PER HOUR, and in a style not excelled by any other process. This simple machine revolutionizes the whole stamping business, by enabling

## EVERY TINSMITH TO PRODUCE HIS OWN STAMPED WORK!

The Machine is NOT COMPLICATED, nor will it get out of order. Any person can fully comprehend it in a few moments. Stands upon the Bench, and takes no more room than a Beading Machine.

☞ Tinsmiths readily concede that it is worth more than the price to make 2 quart Pail Covers only.

EACH MACHINE WARRANTED AS ABOVE.

## PATENT UNIVERSAL TUBE FORMER.

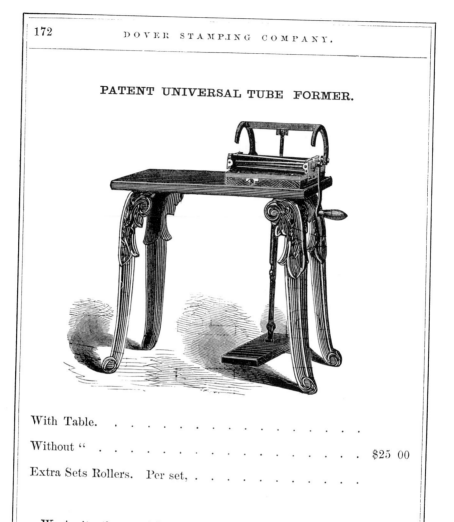

With Table.  .  .  .  .  .  .  .  .  .  .  .  .  .

Without "  .  .  .  .  .  .  .  .  .  .  .  .  $25 00

Extra Sets Rollers.  Per set,  .  .  .  .  .  .  .  .  .

We invite the special attention of the Trade to this most desirable Machine. Its execution is RAPID BEYOND DESCRIPTION, doing more than TWENTY TIMES the labor of the old method, in a given time. The work receives *no scratch*, nor is the surface of the tin changed by passing through the machine.

Candle Moulds, Dipper Handles, Speaking or other Tubing, formed in the same machine. Is easily adjusted to different size tubes.

## SPAULDING'S PATENT DOUBLE SEAMER.

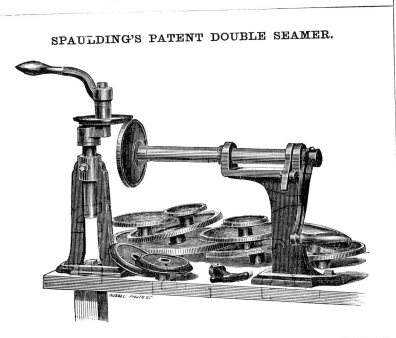

The only machine that will properly DOUBLE SEAM COFFEE POTS, and other FLARING WORK.

This DOUBLE SEAMER commends itself to all workmen upon REGULAR GOODS. Its SIMPLICITY and PERFECT WORK make it more desirable than any other. All ordinary TIN WORK, such as

COFFEE-POTS, or other flaring work,

MILK-PANS, CANS,

PAILS, DIPPERS,

WASH-BASINS, &c

can be DOUBLE SEAMED far MORE RAPIDLY, very MUCH BETTER, and by workmen who have had

### LITTLE OR NO EXPERIENCE.

The objection to other machines — that it takes too long a time to learn to operate them — is done away in this. A new hand will take hold and work it at once.

For COFFEE POTS alone, this machine is worth far more than its cost.

A SINGLE TURN OF THE CRANK, when IC tin is used, completes the seam. Hence its rapidity.

DOVER STAMPING COMPANY,

*88 & 90 North Street, Boston.*

## SANDERSON'S PATENT
# AERO-GAS FIRE POT,

NO
SMOKE.

NO
SMELL.

FOR HEATING
## TINSMITH'S SOLDER COPPERS,
### AND KINDRED PURPOSES.

Plumbers, Braziers, Gas Fitters, Tool Temperers, Silver Platers, Dentists, and others, will find it more PRACTICAL, ECONOMICAL, CLEANLY AND DURABLE than anything of the kind ever invented.

The peculiar *combination* and *concentration* of Air and Gas in this furnace, brings it under perfect control, and renders it practically available for a great variety of purposes where a temperature not above 3500 degrees, Fahrenheit, is needed.

To heat a pair of ordinary Solder Coppers in three minutes, costs with *this* furnace, 1 mill; to heat the same in 20 minutes with charcoal, costs 20 mills! In *this* its GREAT ECONOMY is apparent.

Economy in time — it is ALWAYS READY FOR USE — *no time lost in making a fire.*

Economy in Insurance — *the risk is nothing* — WHEN THE WORK IS DONE THE FIRE IS OUT.

Tinsmiths and others who will take the trouble to examine this invention, will decide that they

CANNOT AFFORD TO BE WITHOUT IT.

We recommend it to Tinsmiths, and for similar purposes, for its great PRACTICAL UTILITY — GREAT ECONOMY, READINESS, CLEANLINESS, and SAFETY.

☞ See Directions on next page.

# DIRECTIONS

### FOR SETTING AT WORK THE

# GAS FIRE POT.

————◆————

Be sure of an AMPLE SUPPLY OF GAS, and see that the connecting pipe is of *sufficient size*, and the *Stop Cocks clear* — to admit it. Connect with either flexible or metal pipe.

Remove the cover of the Fire Pot. Turn on a *full head* of gas, and light at top of burner, and replace the cover. *There must be no flame below the top of the burner.* If the gas be poor, and supply insufficient, the blaze *may* drop to the bottom, inside of the burner, and burn with a flame of less intensity — not unlike that of a burner for *lighting* purposes; in which case, *turn off* the gas, and begin again. If it still persists in dropping down — and burning below the top — the *sides* of the top of the burner must be pressed together — a very little — just enough to remedy the difficulty.

Any flame like that used for lighting purposes *will not do* — for lack of heat.

The RIGHT FLAME is BLUE at the BASE — and CHERRY RED at the TOP — the BLUE part reaching to within about a half inch of the article to be heated.

The quality, richness and pressure of gas being different in different places — the adjustment of the burner must be left to him who uses it. All are made to work perfectly with Boston gas. By a little attention, they will work *anywhere*.

☞ *See that the Burner regulations of the Gas Company are complied with in setting this furnace.*

The estimates are based upon gas at $3.25 per 1000 feet, and charcoal at 40 cents per basket.

Satisfactory testimonials and references sent to those who require them.

## DOVER STAMPING COMPANY,

### *BOSTON.*

## TINNERS' FIRE POT.

FOR CHARCOAL.

DIAMETER, 8 INCHES.

HEIGHT, 14¼ "

The Draft is in the rear of the bottom, and the Fire Pot may be kept full of charcoal without burning higher than is required to heat the coppers. This ensures the *greatest possible economy*.

Top and Bottom, Cast Iron, Body, Sheet Iron. Lined with Fire Brick.

**FIRE POT COMPLETE.** } Each, , . . .

**FIRE POT CASTINGS and BRICK.** } Per Set, . . .

**FIRE POT BRICK.** } Per Set, , . .

# ROYS & WILCOX COMPANY.

## TOOLS AND MACHINES.

### FOLDING MACHINE.

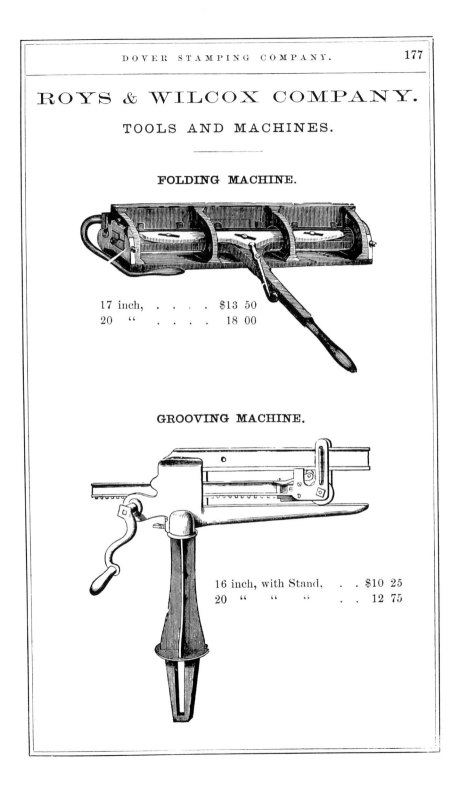

17 inch, . . . . $13 50
20 " . . . . 18 00

### GROOVING MACHINE.

16 inch, with Stand, . . $10 25
20 " " " . . 12 75

## WIRING MACHINE.            SETTING DOWN MACHINE.

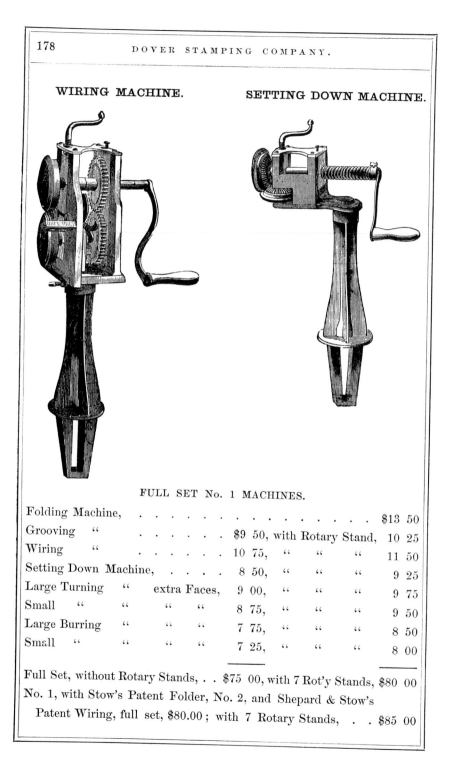

### FULL SET No. 1 MACHINES.

| | | | |
|---|---|---|---|
| Folding Machine, . . . . . . . . . . . . . | | | $13 50 |
| Grooving " . . . . . . | $9 50, with Rotary Stand, | | 10 25 |
| Wiring " . . . . . | 10 75, " " " | | 11 50 |
| Setting Down Machine, . . . . | 8 50, " " " | | 9 25 |
| Large Turning " extra Faces, | 9 00, " " " | | 9 75 |
| Small " " " " | 8 75, " " " | | 9 50 |
| Large Burring " " " | 7 75, " " " | | 8 50 |
| Small " " " " | 7 25, " " " | | 8 00 |

Full Set, without Rotary Stands, . . $75 00, with 7 Rot'y Stands, $80 00

No. 1, with Stow's Patent Folder, No. 2, and Shepard & Stow's
  Patent Wiring, full set, $80.00 ; with 7 Rotary Stands, . . $85 00

## BEADING MACHINES.

WITH WROUGHT IRON ROLLERS,

Converted by a new process to Steel, and warranted to be as hard and durable as Cast Steel.

| | | | | | |
|---|---|---|---|---|---|
| No. 1, Improved, 1 pr. Rolls, 13 in., | . . . . . . . . | $23 00 |
| " 1, Common, " " 12 in., | . . . . . . . . | 21 00 |
| " 2, Improved, " " 10 in., | . . . . . . . . | 22 00 |
| " 3, Improved, " " | . . . . . . . . | 18 00 |
| " 3, Common, " " | . . . . . . . . | 17 00 |
| " 4, Improved, " " for Tin, | . . . . . . . . | 12 00 |
| " 5, Improved, " " for Tin, | . . . . . . . . | 10 00 |
| Extra Wrought Iron Rollers | | |
| Per pair, to Nos. 1 & 2, | . . . . . . . . | 3 50 |
| " " " No. 3, | . . . . . . . . | 3 00 |
| " " " " 4, | . . . . . . . . | 2 00 |
| " " " " 5, | . . . . . . . . | 1 25 |
| Standards for Nos. 1, 2 & 3, each, | . . . . . . . . | 1 25 |
| " " " 4 & 5 " | . . . . . . . . | 75 |

### BEADING MACHINES, — Continued.

The impressions given are $1\frac{1}{8}$ in., 1 in., $\frac{7}{8}$ in., $\frac{1}{2}$ round, O. G. Coffee Pot, Cullender, Elbow, Astragal, and any other form required.

The improved Beading Machine brings the work toward the operator. The Common Beaders carry it from him.

### TIN PIPE FORMER.

### FORMING MACHINES.

No. 00, Extra Large, for heavy Plate, Double Geared, 3 in. Rolls,
　　 37 inches long, . . . . . . . . . . . . . . . . $60 00
" 　0, for Cans, &c., 2 inch Rolls, 37 inches long, . . . . . 24 00
" 　1, Stove Pipe, 　2 　" 　　30 　　" 　. . . . . 19 00
" 　2, 　　" 　　$1\frac{3}{4}$ 　" 　　30 　　" 　. . . . . 18 00
" 　1, Tin Pipe, 　$1\frac{1}{2}$ 　" 　　20 　　" 　. . . . . 10 00
" 　2, 　　" 　　$1\frac{1}{4}$ 　" 　　16 　　" 　. . . . . 9 00
Blacking, Pepper, or Rattle-Box, and Candlestick Former and
　　 Beader, Steel Rods, . . . . . . . . . . . . . . 18 00
Jacket Lamp Former, . . . . . . . . . . . . . . . 20 00
Canister Top, . . . . . . . . . . . . . . . . . 20 00
Candle Mould and Dipper Handle Former, . . . . . . . 16 00
" 　　" 　　Tip 　　　　" 　. . . . . . . 15 00
Iron Frame for Stove Pipe, 　　　" 　. . . . . . . 5 00

# CRIMPING MACHINE.

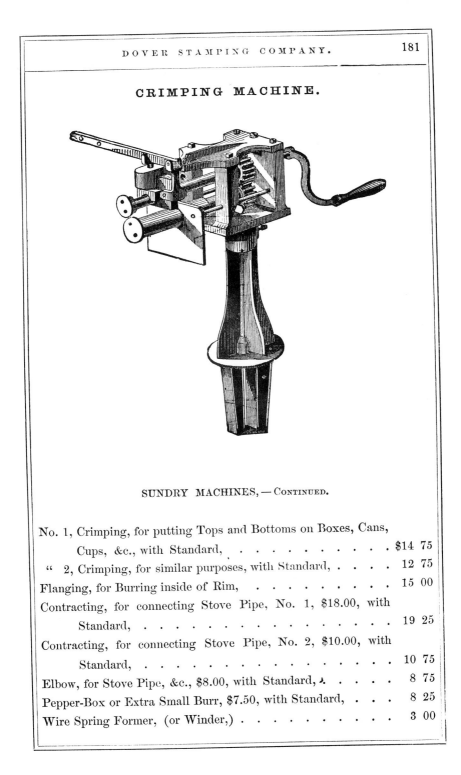

## SUNDRY MACHINES, — Continued.

No. 1, Crimping, for putting Tops and Bottoms on Boxes, Cans,
Cups, &c., with Standard, . . . . . . . . . . . $14 75

" 2, Crimping, for similar purposes, with Standard, . . . . 12 75

Flanging, for Burring inside of Rim, . . . . . . . . . 15 00

Contracting, for connecting Stove Pipe, No. 1, $18.00, with
Standard, . . . . . . . . . . . . . . . . 19 25

Contracting, for connecting Stove Pipe, No. 2, $10.00, with
Standard, . . . . . . . . . . . . . . . . 10 75

Elbow, for Stove Pipe, &c., $8.00, with Standard, . . . . . 8 75

Pepper-Box or Extra Small Burr, $7.50, with Standard, . . . 8 25

Wire Spring Former, (or Winder,) . . . . . . . . . . 3 00

## O. W. STOW'S PATENT FOLDING MACHINE.

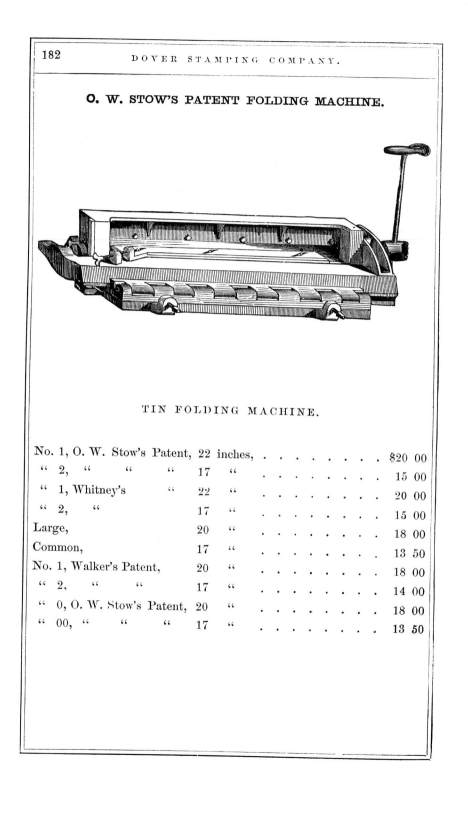

## TIN FOLDING MACHINE.

| | | | |
|---|---|---|---|
| No. 1, O. W. Stow's Patent, | 22 inches, | . . . . . . . . | $20 00 |
| " 2, " " " | 17 " | . . . . . . . . | 15 00 |
| " 1, Whitney's " | 22 " | . . . . . . . . | 20 00 |
| " 2, " | 17 " | . . . . . . . . | 15 00 |
| Large, | 20 " | . . . . . . . . | 18 00 |
| Common, | 17 " | . . . . . . . . | 13 50 |
| No. 1, Walker's Patent, | 20 " | . . . . . . . . | 18 00 |
| " 2, " " | 17 " | . . . . . . . . | 14 00 |
| " 0, O. W. Stow's Patent, | 20 " | . . . . . . . . | 18 00 |
| " 00, " " " | 17 " | . . . . . . . . | 13 50 |

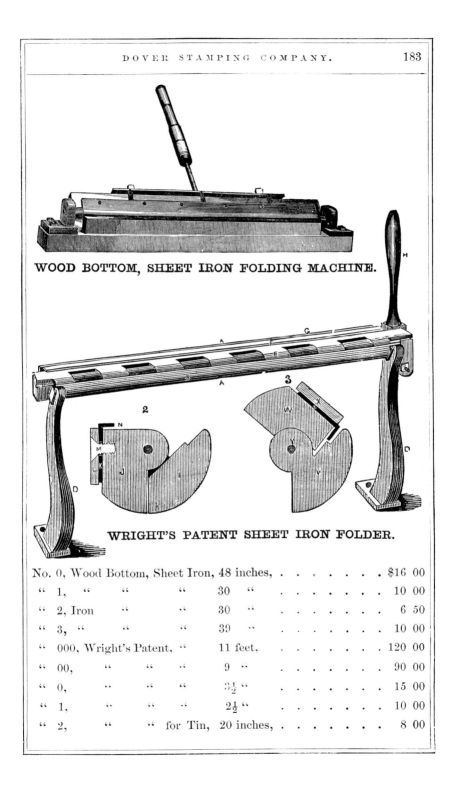

**WOOD BOTTOM, SHEET IRON FOLDING MACHINE.**

**WRIGHT'S PATENT SHEET IRON FOLDER.**

| | | | | | |
|---|---|---|---|---|---|
| No. 0, Wood Bottom, Sheet Iron, 48 inches, . . . . . . . | $16 00 |
| " 1, " " " 30 " . . . . . . . | 10 00 |
| " 2, Iron " " 30 " . . . . . . . | 6 50 |
| " 3, " " " 39 " . . . . . . . | 10 00 |
| " 000, Wright's Patent, " 11 feet, . . . . . . . | 120 00 |
| " 00, " " " 9 " . . . . . . . | 90 00 |
| " 0, " " " 3½ " . . . . . . . | 15 00 |
| " 1, " " " 2¼ " . . . . . . . | 10 00 |
| " 2, " " for Tin, 20 inches, . . . . . . . | 8 00 |

## O. W. STOW'S TUBE FORMER.—NO. 1.

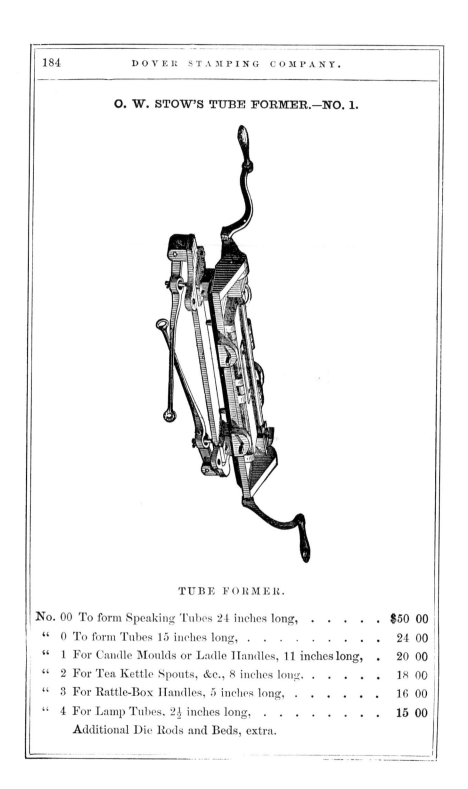

### TUBE FORMER.

No. 00  To form Speaking Tubes 24 inches long,  . . . . .  **$50 00**

"   0  To form Tubes 15 inches long,  . . . . . . . .   24 00

"   1  For Candle Moulds or Ladle Handles, 11 inches long,  .   20 00

"   2  For Tea Kettle Spouts, &c., 8 inches long. . . . . .   18 00

"   3  For Rattle-Box Handles, 5 inches long, . . . . . .   16 00

"   4  For Lamp Tubes, 2½ inches long,  . . . . . . . .   **15 00**

Additional Die Rods and Beds, extra.

## SQUARE BOX FOLDING MACHINE.

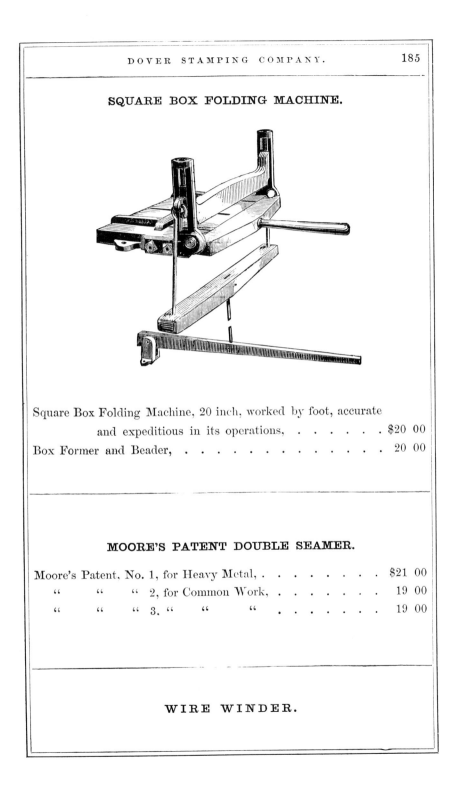

Square Box Folding Machine, 20 inch, worked by foot, accurate
and expeditious in its operations, . . . . . . . $20 00
Box Former and Beader, . . . . . . . . . . . . . 20 00

## MOORE'S PATENT DOUBLE SEAMER.

Moore's Patent, No. 1, for Heavy Metal, . . . . . . . . . $21 00
" " " 2, for Common Work, . . . . . . . . 19 00
" " " 3, " " " . . . . . . . 19 00

## WIRE WINDER.

## STOW'S PATTERN SQUARING SHEARS.

FOR CUTTING SHEET METALS, &C.

These Shears are arranged with Gauges for Squaring, Stripping and Cutting at any desired angle, without the necessity of marking the sheet, and doing the work much quicker.

No. 0, are for cutting Sheets (30 inches) of Heavy Metal, Steel, Iron, Brass or Copper.

No. 1, are for cutting Sheet Iron, &c.: No. 2, for Tin and other light metals.

No. 00, R. & W. Co. Pattern with iron frame, cut 37 in., . . . $125 00
"  0,     "     "     "     "     " 30 " . . . 120 00
"  1, R. & W., or P. S. Co. pat'n with iron frame, cut 30 in.,  $47 00
"  1,     "     "     "   " without "     " 30 "   40 00
"  2,     "     "     "   " with "     " 20 "   32 00
"  2,     "     "     "   " without "     " 20 "   26 00
"  1, Stow's Pattern,       " with "     " 30 "   50 00
"  2,     "     "       " with "     " 20 "   35 00
Extra Blades, No. 2,     Per Pair, . . . . . . . . . $9 00
"     "     " 1,     "   " . . . . . . . . . 12 00
"     "     Nos. 0 & 00, "   " . . . . . . . . . 16 00

Lever Shears of any desired length, (for cutting straight work) made to order.

## ROYS & WILCOX CO'S PATTERN SQUARING SHEARS.

FOR CUTTING SHEET METALS, PAPER, &C.

A GREAT LABOR-SAVING MACHINE.

The subscribers now offer to manufacturers, and dealers in Tin Plate and Sheet Iron, a Machine that after many years' experimenting, we have no hesitation in recommending as the *Best Shears* for cutting Sheet Metals into Strips, square, or at any angle, that has ever been offered to the public. The operator having *both* hands at liberty to manage the Sheets, can cut more work, with greater accuracy, and much less grinding to keep them in order, than with any other Shears. They are made wholly of Steel and Iron, and are *strong and durable*, easily worked, (by the foot,) and not liable to get out of repair by being worked by inexperienced hands.

ROYS & WILCOX CO.

## FLANDERS' PATENT
## IMPROVED CIRCULAR OR ROTARY SHEARS,

### FOR CUTTING AND BENDING.

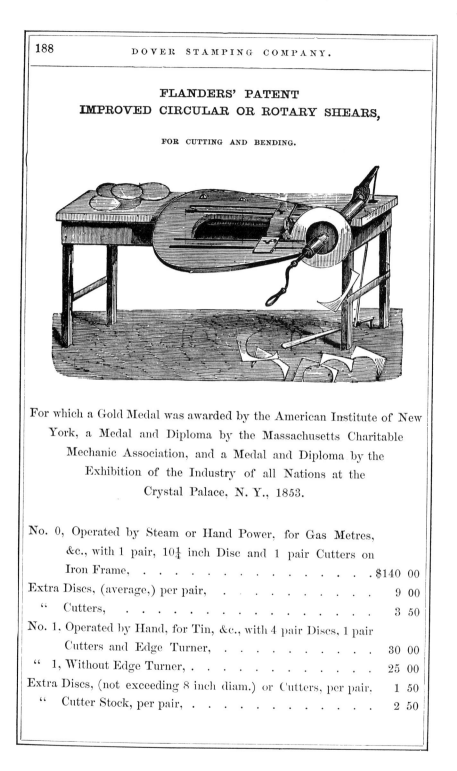

For which a Gold Medal was awarded by the American Institute of New York, a Medal and Diploma by the Massachusetts Charitable Mechanic Association, and a Medal and Diploma by the Exhibition of the Industry of all Nations at the Crystal Palace, N. Y., 1853.

No. 0, Operated by Steam or Hand Power, for Gas Metres, &c., with 1 pair, 10¼ inch Disc and 1 pair Cutters on Iron Frame, . . . . . . . . . . . . . . . . . . $140 00

Extra Discs, (average,) per pair, . . . . . . . . . 9 00

" Cutters, . . . . . . . . . . . . . . . 3 50

No. 1, Operated by Hand, for Tin, &c., with 4 pair Discs, 1 pair Cutters and Edge Turner, . . . . . . . . . . . 30 00

" 1, Without Edge Turner, . . . . . . . . . . . . 25 00

Extra Discs, (not exceeding 8 inch diam.) or Cutters, per pair. 1 50

" Cutter Stock, per pair, . . . . . . . . . . . . 2 50

## O. W. STOW'S IMPROVED GUTTER BEADER.

## NO. 3, IRON BOTTOM GUTTER BEADER.

### GUTTER MACHINES.

| | | | |
|---|---|---|---|
| No. 0, with 2 Wood Rolls, $\frac{5}{8}$ Cast Steel Rod, 20 inch, . . . . | $5 00 |
| " 1, " " " " $\frac{5}{8}$ " " 15 " . . . . | 4 50 |
| " 2, Iron Bottom, $\frac{3}{8}$ or $\frac{1}{2}$ " " 20 " . . . . | 4 00 |
| " 3, " " $\frac{3}{8}$ or $\frac{1}{2}$ " " 15 " . . . . | 3 50 |
| " 1, O. W. Stow's Improved, " 20 " . . . . | 5 50 |
| " 2, " " " 15 " . . . . | 4 50 |
| " 1. Steel Gutter Rods, 20 " . . . . | 2 00 |
| " 2, " " " 14 " . . . . | 1 75 |

## BENCH SHEARS.

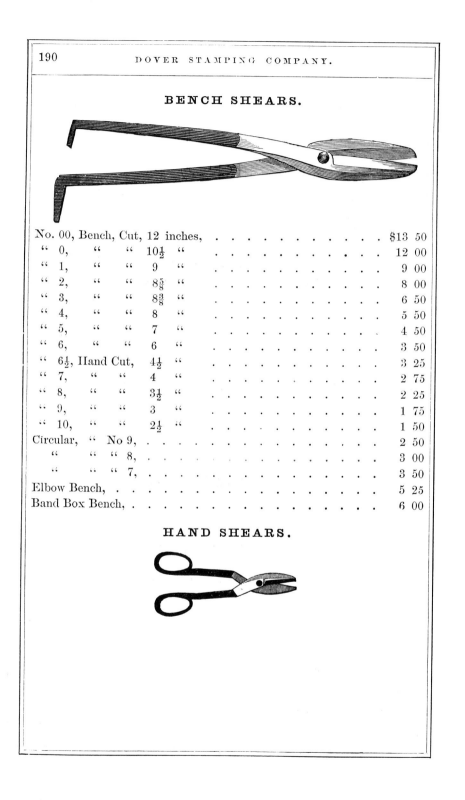

| | | | | | |
|---|---|---|---|---|---|
| No. 00, Bench, Cut, 12 inches, | . . . . . . . . . . | $13 50 |
| " 0, " " 10½ " | . . . . . . . . . | 12 00 |
| " 1, " " 9 " | . . . . . . . . . | 9 00 |
| " 2, " " 8⅝ " | . . . . . . . . . | 8 00 |
| " 3, " " 8¾ " | . . . . . . . . . | 6 50 |
| " 4, " " 8 " | . . . . . . . . . | 5 50 |
| " 5, " " 7 " | . . . . . . . . . | 4 50 |
| " 6, " " 6 " | . . . . . . . . . | 3 50 |
| " 6½, Hand Cut, 4½ " | . . . . . . . . . | 3 25 |
| " 7, " " 4 " | . . . . . . . . . | 2 75 |
| " 8, " " 3½ " | . . . . . . . . . | 2 25 |
| " 9, " " 3 " | . . . . . . . . . | 1 75 |
| " 10, " " 2½ " | . . . . . . . . . | 1 50 |
| Circular, " No 9, . | . . . . . . . . . | 2 50 |
| " " " 8, | . . . . . . . . . | 3 00 |
| " " " 7, | . . . . . . . . . | 3 50 |
| Elbow Bench, . | . . . . . . . . . | 5 25 |
| Band Box Bench, . | . . . . . . . . . | 6 00 |

## HAND SHEARS.

## HOLLOW PUNCH.　　SET SOLID PUNCHES.

### HOLLOW PUNCHES.

All sizes to and including 1¾ inch diameter, Round, per inch, . . $1 00

All sizes above 1¾ " " " " . . 1 25

Oval. per inch, . . . . . . . . . 1 50

### CAST STEEL CHISELS.

Circular, per inch, . . . . . . . . . . . . . . . . . $0 25

Lantern, Common Size, . . . . . . . . . . . . . . . 12

Wire, . . . . $\frac{1}{4}—\frac{1}{2}—\frac{5}{8}—\frac{3}{4}—\frac{7}{8}—1—1\frac{1}{8}—1\frac{1}{4}—1\frac{1}{2}—1\frac{3}{4}—2$ inch.

　　　　　　　8　10　11　12　13　14　15　17　20　24　29 cts.

### SOLID PUNCHES.

Sqr. C. S., No. 0, 1, 2, 3, 4, 5, 6, 7, 8, and Prick, each, . . . $0 12

Round Steel, . . . . . . . . . . . . . . . . . . 10

### BENCH PLATES.

No. 1, Cast Iron, . . . . . . . . . . . . . . . . . $5 00

" 2. " . . . . . . . . . . . . . . . . 3 00

## BEAKHORN STAKE.

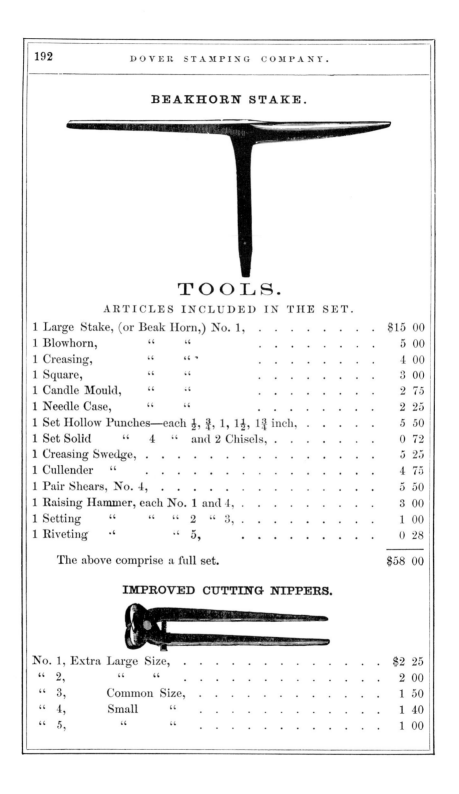

# TOOLS.

### ARTICLES INCLUDED IN THE SET.

| | | |
|---|---|---:|
| 1 Large Stake, (or Beak Horn,) No. 1, | . . . . . . . | $15 00 |
| 1 Blowhorn, " " | . . . . . . . . | 5 00 |
| 1 Creasing, " " ' | . . . . . . . . | 4 00 |
| 1 Square, " " | . . . . . . . . | 3 00 |
| 1 Candle Mould, " " | . . . . . . . . | 2 75 |
| 1 Needle Case, " " | . . . . . . . . | 2 25 |
| 1 Set Hollow Punches—each $\frac{1}{2}$, $\frac{3}{4}$, 1, $1\frac{1}{2}$, $1\frac{3}{4}$ inch, | . . . . . | 5 50 |
| 1 Set Solid " 4 " and 2 Chisels, | . . . . . . . | 0 72 |
| 1 Creasing Swedge, | . . . . . . . . . . . | 5 25 |
| 1 Cullender " | . . . . . . . . . . | 4 75 |
| 1 Pair Shears, No. 4, | . . . . . . . . . . . | 5 50 |
| 1 Raising Hammer, each No. 1 and 4, | . . . . . . . | 3 00 |
| 1 Setting " " " 2 " 3, | . . . . . . . . | 1 00 |
| 1 Riveting " " 5, | . . . . . . . . | 0 28 |

The above comprise a full set.                         $58 00

## IMPROVED CUTTING NIPPERS.

| | | |
|---|---|---:|
| No. 1, Extra Large Size, | . . . . . . . . . . | $2 25 |
| " 2, " " | . . . . . . . . . . . | 2 00 |
| " 3, Common Size, | . . . . . . . . . . | 1 50 |
| " 4, Small " | . . . . . . . . . | 1 40 |
| " 5, " " | . . . . . . . . . . | 1 00 |

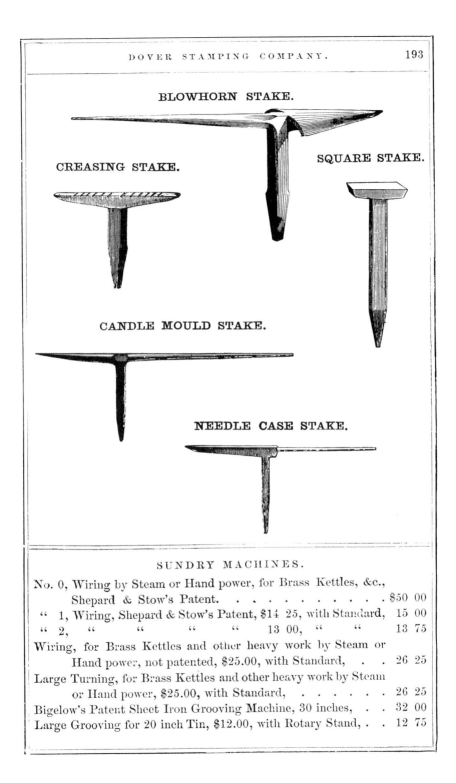

BLOWHORN STAKE.

CREASING STAKE.

SQUARE STAKE.

CANDLE MOULD STAKE.

NEEDLE CASE STAKE.

### SUNDRY MACHINES.

No. 0, Wiring by Steam or Hand power, for Brass Kettles, &c.,
    Shepard & Stow's Patent. . . . . . . . . . .$50 00
" 1, Wiring, Shepard & Stow's Patent, $14 25, with Standard, 15 00
" 2,   "     "     "     "   13 00, "     "   13 75
Wiring, for Brass Kettles and other heavy work by Steam or
    Hand power, not patented, $25.00, with Standard,  . . 26 25
Large Turning, for Brass Kettles and other heavy work by Steam
    or Hand power, $25.00, with Standard,  . . . . . 26 25
Bigelow's Patent Sheet Iron Grooving Machine, 30 inches,  . . 32 00
Large Grooving for 20 inch Tin, $12.00, with Rotary Stand, . . 12 75

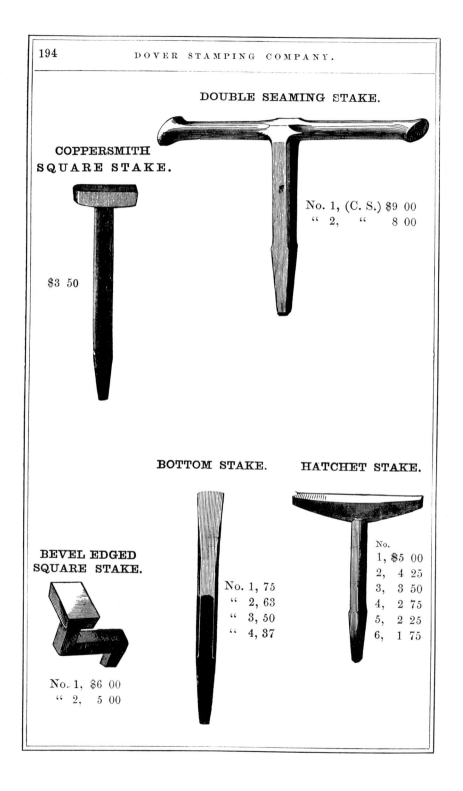

**DOUBLE SEAMING STAKE.**

**COPPERSMITH SQUARE STAKE.**

No. 1, (C. S.) $9 00
" 2, " 8 00

$3 50

**BOTTOM STAKE.**　**HATCHET STAKE.**

**BEVEL EDGED SQUARE STAKE.**

No.
1, $5 00
2, 4 25
3, 3 50
4, 2 75
5, 2 25
6, 1 75

No. 1, 75
" 2, 63
" 3, 50
" 4, 37

No. 1, $6 00
" 2, 5 00

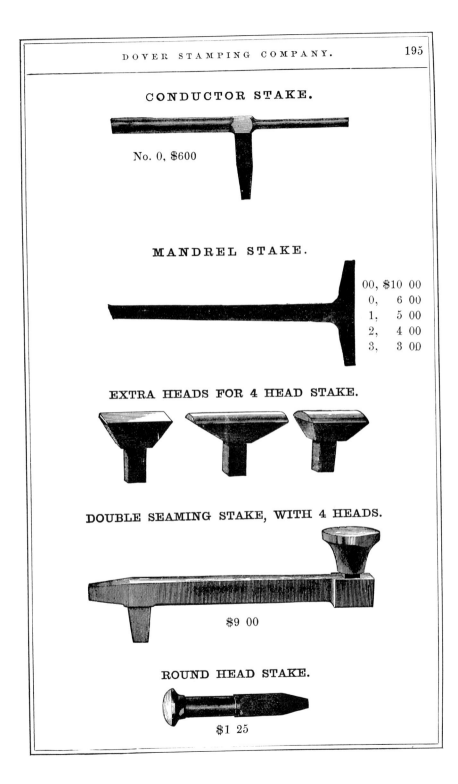

## CONDUCTOR STAKE.

No. 0, $600

## MANDREL STAKE.

00, $10 00
0, 6 00
1, 5 00
2, 4 00
3, 3 00

## EXTRA HEADS FOR 4 HEAD STAKE.

## DOUBLE SEAMING STAKE, WITH 4 HEADS.

$9 00

## ROUND HEAD STAKE.

$1 25

## STAKES.

No. 1, Large (or Beak Horn,) 45 lbs., . . . . . . . . . . $15 00
"  2,  "          "          40 " . . . . . . . . . 13 25
"  3,  "          "          35 " . . . . . . . . . 11 50
"  4,  "          "          30 " . . . . . . . . . 10 00
"  1, Double Seaming, large end 16 inches, small end 11 inches,  9 00
"  2,  "          "          each end 11 inches, . . . . . . . 8 00
"  0, Conductor, each end 14 inches, . . . . . . . . . 6 00
"  1, Bevel Edged Square,  . . . . . . . . . . . . 6 00
"  2,  "          "          "          . . . . . . . . . . 5 00
Common Blowhorn,  . . . . . . . . . . . . . . . 5 00
Creasing with Horn, . . . . . . . . . . . . . . . 4 50
Common Creasing,  . . . . . . . . . . . . . . . 4 00
Coppersmith Square, . . . . . . . . . . . . . . . 3 50
Common        "          . . . . . . . . . . . . . . 3 00
Candle Mould, . . . . . . . . . . . . . . . . . 2 75
Needle Case,  . . . . . . . . . . . . . . . . . 2 25
Small Square, . . . . . . . . . . . . . . . . . 1 25
Tea Kettle, Wrought Iron Standard,  . . . . . . . . . 8 75
Heads for do., each, Cast Steel,  . . . . . . . . . . 1 75
No. 1, Hatchet, blade 16 inches long,  . . . . . . . . . 5 00
"  2,  "          "     14½  " . . . . . . . . . . 4 25
"  3,  "          "     13   " . . . . . . . . . . 3 50
"  4,  "          "     11   " . . . . . . . . . . 2 75
"  5,  "          "      9   " . . . . . . . . . . 2 25
"  6,  "          "      7   " . . . . . . . . . . 1 75
"  1, Bottom, Width 1¾ inch,  . . . . . . . . . . 75
"  2,  "          "     1½  " . . . . . . . . . . 63
"  3,  "          "     1¼  " . . . . . . . . . . 50
"  4,  "          "     1   " . . . . . . . . . . 37

## STAKES—Continued.

### CAST IRON.

HOLLOW MANDREL STAKE.

| | | |
|---|---|---:|
| No.  1, Conductor, Turned, | . . . . | $4 00 |
| "   2,   "            " | . . . . | 3 00 |
| "   00, Mandrel, 5 feet long, | . . . . | 10 00 |
| "   0,   "    3  "   4 inches, | . . | 6 00 |
| "   1,   "    2  "  10  " | . . | 5 00 |
| "   2,   "    2  "   6  " | . . | 4 00 |
| "   3,   "    2  "   3  " | . . | 3 00 |
| Hollow    " | . . . . . . . | 5 50 |
| Grooving,  " | . . . . . . . | 5 50 |
| Boiler,    " | . . . . . . . | 5 00 |
| Double Seaming, with 4 Heads, | . . . | 9 00 |
| Extra Heads for do., | . . . . . . . | 1 50 |
| Common Beak Horn, | . . . . . . | 7 00 |
| "      Double Seaming, | . . . . | 5 00 |
| Bevel Edged Square, | . . . . . . . | 2 50 |
| Round Head, | . . . . . . . | 1 25 |
| Candle Mould Square, | . . . . . . | 0 75 |
| Bath Tub, | . . . . . . . . . | 1 25 |

## BATH TUB STAKE.

## RIVET SET AND HEADERS.

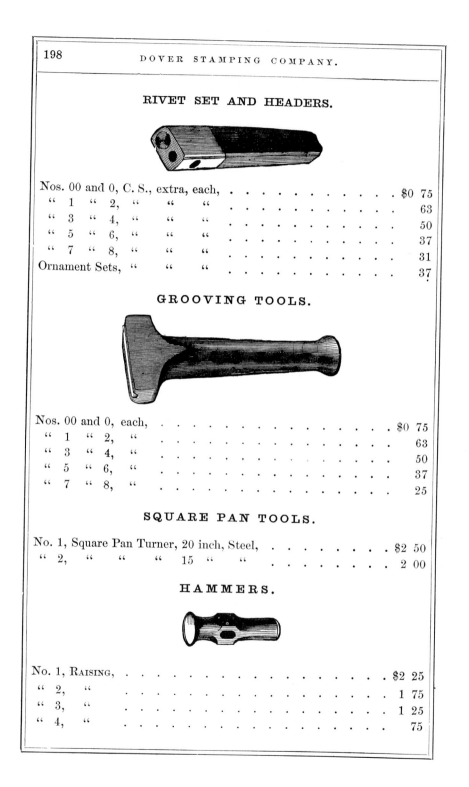

| | |
|---|---|
| Nos. 00 and 0, C. S., extra, each, . . . . . . . . . . . . . | $0 75 |
| "    1    "    2,    "        "        " . . . . . . . . . . . . | 63 |
| "    3    "    4,    "        "        " . . . . . . . . . . . . | 50 |
| "    5    "    6,    "        "        " . . . . . . . . . . . . | 37 |
| "    7    "    8,    "        "        " . . . . . . . . . . . . | 31 |
| Ornament Sets,    "        "        " . . . . . . . . . . . . | 37 |

## GROOVING TOOLS.

| | |
|---|---|
| Nos. 00 and 0,  each, . . . . . . . . . . . . . . . . . . . | $0 75 |
| "    1    "    2,    " . . . . . . . . . . . . . . . . . . | 63 |
| "    3    "    4,    " . . . . . . . . . . . . . . . . . . | 50 |
| "    5    "    6,    " . . . . . . . . . . . . . . . . . . | 37 |
| "    7    "    8,    " . . . . . . . . . . . . . . . . . . | 25 |

## SQUARE PAN TOOLS.

| | |
|---|---|
| No. 1, Square Pan Turner, 20 inch, Steel, . . . . . . . . . | $2 50 |
| "   2,     "      "      "    15   "      " . . . . . . . . . | 2 00 |

## HAMMERS.

| | |
|---|---|
| No. 1, RAISING, . . . . . . . . . . . . . . . . . . | $2 25 |
| "    2,    " . . . . . . . . . . . . . . . . . . . . | 1 75 |
| "    3,    " . . . . . . . . . . . . . . . . . . . . | 1 25 |
| "    4,    " . . . . . . . . . . . . . . . . . . . . | 75 |

## HAMMERS.—Continued.

| | | | | | | | |
|---|---|---|---|---|---|---|---|
| No. 0, RIVETING, | Heavy Work, Bright, 1½ in., . | | with Handles, | $0 93 |
| " 1, | " | Sheet Iron, | " | C. S., 1⅛ in., | " | " | 82 |
| " 2, | " | Tin, &c., | " | 1 " " | " | 70 |
| " 3, | " | " | " | ⅞ " " | " | 56 |
| " 4, | " | " | " | ¾ " " | " | 45 |
| " 5, | " | " | " | ⅝ " " | " | 40 |
| " 0, | " | Heavy Work, Black, | | 1½ " " | " | 81 |
| " 1, | " | Sheet Iron, | " | 1⅛ " " | " | 75 |
| " 2, | " | Tin, &c., | " | 1 " " | " | 63 |
| " 3, | " | " | " | ⅞ " " | " | 50 |
| " 4, | " | " | .. | ¾ " " | " | 40 |
| " 5, | " | " | " | ⅝ " " | " | 35 |

| | | | | | | |
|---|---|---|---|---|---|---|
| No. 1, SETTING, Bright, C. S., 1⅛ in., with Handles, | . . . . | $0 81 |
| " 2, | " | " | " | 1 " " " | . . . . | 70 |
| " 3, | " | " | " | ⅞ " " " | . . . . | 56 |
| " 4, | " | " | " | ¾ " " " | . . . . | 45 |
| " 5, | " | " | " | ⅝ " " " | . . . . | 40 |
| " 1, | " | Black, | | 1⅛ " " " | . . . . | 75 |
| " 2, | " | " | | 1 " " " | . . . . | 62 |
| " 3, | " | " | | ⅞ " " " | . . . . | 50 |
| " 4, | " | " | | ¾ " " " | . . . . | 40 |
| " 5, | " | " | | ⅝ " " " | . . . . | 35 |

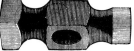

| | |
|---|---|
| Planishing, per lb., . . . . . . . . . . . . . . . . | $1 00 |
| Cast Iron Raising, No. 1, . . . . . . . . . . . . . | 1 00 |
| " " " 2, . . . . . . . . . . . . | 75 |
| " " " 3, . . . . . . . . . . . . | 50 |
| " " " 4, . . . . . . . . . . . . | 38 |
| Handled, per dozen, extra, . . . . . . . . . . . . | 75 |

## CREASING SWEDGE.

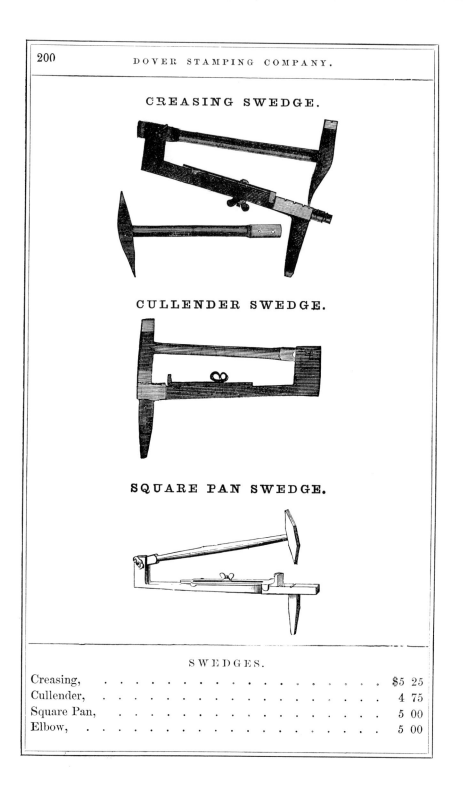

## CULLENDER SWEDGE.

## SQUARE PAN SWEDGE.

### SWEDGES.

| | |
|---|---|
| Creasing, | $5 25 |
| Cullender, | 4 75 |
| Square Pan, | 5 00 |
| Elbow, | 5 00 |

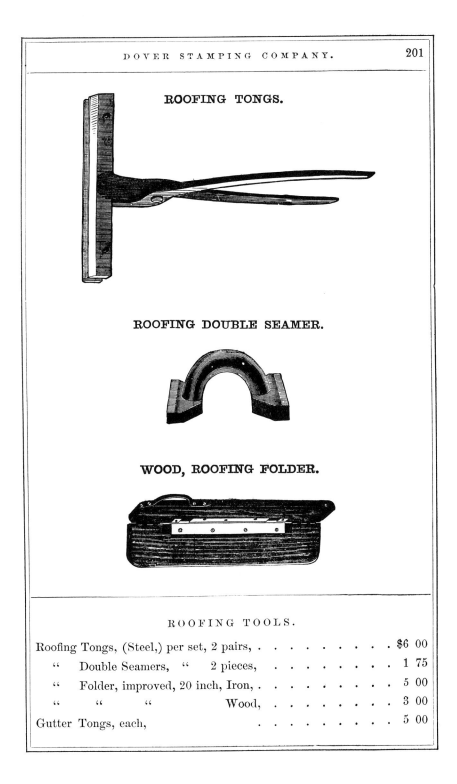

## ROOFING TONGS.

## ROOFING DOUBLE SEAMER.

## WOOD, ROOFING FOLDER.

ROOFING TOOLS.

Roofing Tongs, (Steel,) per set, 2 pairs, . . . . . . . . . $6 00
   "     Double Seamers,    "     2 pieces,   . . . . . . . . 1 75
   "     Folder, improved, 20 inch, Iron, . . . . . . . . . 5 00
   "    "    "     Wood,   . . . . . . . . 3 00
Gutter Tongs, each,         . . . . . . . . . 5 00

We take pleasure in calling the attention of our friends and customers to the NEW PATENT MACHINES manufactured by the S. STOW MANUFACTURING COMPANY, a supply of which we have constantly on hand.

---

# S T O W ' S
# TOOLS AND MACHINES,

### O. W. STOW'S NEW PAT. OF 1867, WITH

## A D J U S T A B L E   B O X E S

#### AND DUPLICATE PARTS.

The prices annexed are subject to an advance at the present time.

## IMPROVED GROOVING MACHINE.

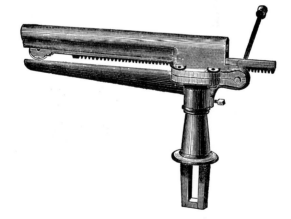

Common, . . 17 inches, $9 50, with Rotary Stand, . . $10 25
For heavy work, 20 " 12 00, " " " . . 12 75

We have recently greatly improved our Grooving Machine, and it will be found in every particular superior to that of other manufacturers.

## O. W. STOW'S PATENT ADJUSTABLE BAR FOLDER.

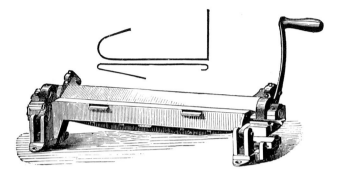

This simple and admirable machine is decidedly the best in use. It forms a SQUARE JOINT: turns ROUND EDGES for wiring, and forms LOCKS ON VERY HEAVY PLATE with ease.

No. 0, O. W. Stow's Patent of 1860, 22 inches,  . . . $18 00
" 00, "     "     "     " 17 "   . . . 13 50

### DIRECTIONS FOR USING.

Fasten the machine to the bench by means of small wood screws, with the crank at the right hand.

Place the edge of the sheet of tin under the folding plate, then bring over the folding bar, and the lock is formed. To form a bend at right angles, put the stop A, in such a position as to stop the folding bar from turning more than one quarter of a revolution.

It will be noticed that the folding bar is made in two parts: one of which is adjustable with reference to the folding plate, for the purpose of turning a close or open lock. This feature greatly increases the utility of the machine; for while it will do any work done on any other machine, and will form locks on heavy plate more easily than most others: it will at the same time turn the edges of a sheet of tin to fit wire of any size, so that it will take the place of the turning machines in wiring straight work.

To form a bend to fit wire of any size: set the folding bar so as to press more or less closely, when it is turned over on the plate — this is done by the thumb screw at the right hand of the folding bar. By loosening this thumb screw, and moving from right to left, the folding bar is raised to form a close lock — by moving it from left to right, it is put in position to form an open lock — and these changes can be made with great ease and rapidity. If the jaws do not hold the tin firmly, make them do so by turning the screws in the end of the frame that holds the friction rollers.

Tinsmiths will find it to their interest to purchase this folder.

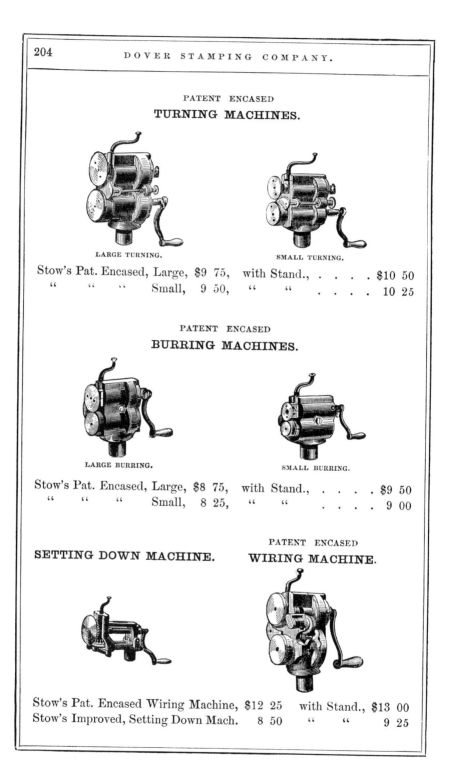

PATENT ENCASED
## TURNING MACHINES.

LARGE TURNING.      SMALL TURNING.

Stow's Pat. Encased, Large, $9 75, with Stand., . . . . $10 50
"    "    "     Small,   9 50,   "     "     . . . .   10 25

PATENT ENCASED
## BURRING MACHINES.

LARGE BURRING.      SMALL BURRING.

Stow's Pat. Encased, Large, $8 75, with Stand., . . . . $9 50
"    "    "     Small,   8 25,   "     "     . . . .   9 00

                              PATENT ENCASED
## SETTING DOWN MACHINE.    WIRING MACHINE.

Stow's Pat. Encased Wiring Machine, $12 25    with Stand., $13 00
Stow's Improved, Setting Down Mach.   8 50    "     "     9 25

## STANDARDS.

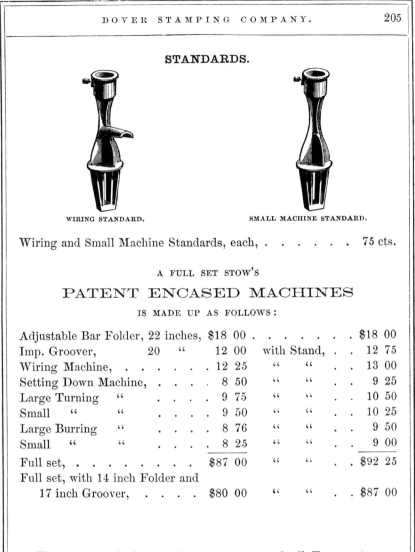

WIRING STANDARD.          SMALL MACHINE STANDARD.

Wiring and Small Machine Standards, each, . . . . . . . 75 cts.

A FULL SET STOW'S

# PATENT ENCASED MACHINES

### IS MADE UP AS FOLLOWS:

| | | | | | |
|---|---|---|---|---|---|
| Adjustable Bar Folder, 22 inches, | $18 00 | . . . . . . . | $18 00 |
| Imp. Groover, 20 " | 12 00 | with Stand, . . | 12 75 |
| Wiring Machine, . . . . . . | 12 25 | " " . . | 13 00 |
| Setting Down Machine, . . . . | 8 50 | " " . . | 9 25 |
| Large Turning " . . . . | 9 75 | " " . . | 10 50 |
| Small " " . . . . | 9 50 | " " . . | 10 25 |
| Large Burring " . . . . | 8 76 | " " . . | 9 50 |
| Small " " . . . . | 8 25 | " " . . | 9 00 |
| Full set, . . . . . . . . | $87 00 | " " . . | $92 25 |
| Full set, with 14 inch Folder and 17 inch Groover, . . . . | $80 00 | " " . . | $87 00 |

The foregoing is the set that we recommend all TINNERS to purchase, as the price of the full set is *only* $5 00 higher than the common set, and they will OUTLAST TWO SETS OF THE ORDINARY MACHINE.

We can, if desired, furnish the old style of machines, made as well as such machines can be manufactured, at the ordinary prices.

# INDEX.

## A

## B

## C

# D

# E

# F

# G

# H

# I

# J

# K

# L

# M

# N

# O

# P

# R

# S

# T

# U

# V

# W

# Y

# DOVER STAMPING COMPANY
## an historical introduction

Well into the early years of this century, the horse-drawn delivery wagons of the Dover Stamping Company were a familiar sight to residents of the Boston area. Along with milk wagons and peddlers' carts, they provided a useful and colorful display of moving commercial enterprise at a time when neighborhood supermarkets and cut-rate hardware stores were non-existent.

Dover sold to the general public and to other distributors. It supplied hundreds of items to peddlers and to stores selling hardware, machines to tinsmiths, and the most basic household wares, stove pipe and tin implements to the home consumer. Sales, however, were not only confined to the Boston or northern New England area. The illustrated catalog, issued annually, was the means by which Dover reached far and wide as a direct-mail supplier. And such was the reputation of the firm that they received thousands of orders by mail each year, orders not unlike the following plea sent from Portland, Oregon, as late as 1952:

"Dear Dover Stamping Co.

I have one of your 'one eggs' beaters with whipping end about 1″ diam. blades. Cannot find one in Portland. Can you send me C.O.D.? My old one is worn out after 40 years."

Few housewives today have ever used a Dover eggbeater. A simple tin and iron model was introduced for the first time in the 1870's. It was an almost instant success. Patented by Dover in 1878 ("The Mother of them All—Guaranteed to Outwear any other Egg Beater made"), it became a staple item in the American kitchen. Fanny Farmer recommended its use, as did other nineteenth-century cookbook authors. Well into the 1930's, Dover salesmen were selling more of the various eggbeater items than almost any other product line.

The ingenuity that went into the manufacture *and* promotion of such times as the eggbeater was of pure Yankee origin. Horace Whitney of Kennebunk, Maine, founded the company in Dover, New Hampshire, in 1833, and remained its President until his death in 1883. Begun as Horace Whitney and Company, the first factory and retail store was in a good-sized red brick building on Dover's Main Street.

Soon a line of cooking stoves was added, and the enterprise became popularly known as the Dover Stove Factory. It is apparent that for the first twenty years the business of the company was limited—both in geographical and economic terms. Stoves were a part of their local business. Stove pipe and other basic tin products such as candle moulds and cutters were offered as well. Slowly the firm's salesmen, in this case Horace Whitney and his son, Edward, established very profitable accounts for their wares. That they founded these accounts on a firm footing and diligently serviced them is testified to in the company's early ledgers. Many of their early customers stayed with them for as long as 75 years!

By 1857 the Whitneys had developed enough business in the Boston market to warrant the opening of an office and warehouse at 67 Blackstone St. Such other stove manufacturers as Moses Pond & Co. and Dighton Furnace Company already had their showrooms in this neighborhood. The opening of a Boston office also facilitated the importation of English tin plate, some of which entered through the port of Boston until the early 1890's when the restrictive McKinley tariff became effective. In 1857 the firm's name was changed to that presently used—Dover Stamping Company.

The Civil War undoubtedly thinned the ranks of the New Hampshire factory workers, but the company itself profited greatly from business engendered by military action. There is no remaining record of how production was increased, but the Whitneys saw to it that a full line of tin cups, cutlery, lanterns and other tin goods were made available to the Union Army. By the end of the war in 1865, the firm was ready to embark on a course of mass production manufacturing and national marketing. Along with much other Northern industry, the war had provided them with the profits and the skills for more ambitious commercial ventures.

The factory and store in Dover were now much too small, and the location too distant from the company's primary urban market—Boston. In 1865 work was begun on a new factory in Cambridge, Massachusetts (then in an area known as Cambridgeport). These impressive new facilities were opened with much fanfare on June 16, 1866.

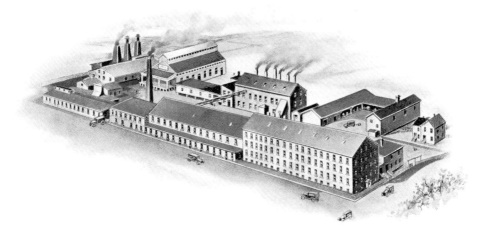

Competition in the Boston area was plentiful. Among the rival firms were C. J. Simonds, C. C. Wood and Co., Lincoln and Hopkinson, and F. A. Walker and Co. Business, however, grew by leaps and bounds during the post-Civil War period. Dover held on to its stove market and greatly increased its share of the domestic housewares field. Until the Civil War, a great deal of this merchandise had been imported from England.

The 1869 catalog abundantly illustrates the many different kinds of product lines which Dover offered. In the same year, the company moved its Boston sales office and warehouse to a larger location at 80-90 North Street, a building pictured in the catalog. A year later Dover was incorporated under the general laws of Massachusetts with Horace Whitney as President.

By 1869 a full line of tin housewares was being offered: plain tinware, Brittania ware, Jappanned ware, then declining in popularity, toilet ware, and French tinned iron goods. As noted in the catalog in a letter "To the Trade," Dover "endeavored to meet a growing demand for a better quality of French Tinned Goods than has hitherto been manufactured in this country, to which end we have made large investments of money, and procured from abroad competent workmen, which we find to have been warranted by the results."

Only a small proportion of the nineteenth-century Dover goods can be considered "decorative," even by the standards applied today to such "antique" items. Clearly, however, the products were turned out with more care, if not precision, than similar items manufactured today. The tinware was more heavily plated than the same products were in the first decades of the present century when they were still in popular use. The extra heavy coating was a special protection from damage.

Many customers wanted "decorative" kitchenware, and they desired more than bright colors. The Japanned and "richly decorated" toilet ware met these needs. The stencilled ware pieces are highly prized today when they *can* be found. Also valued are the tea and coffee pot knobs and the highly ornate stove ornaments. Decoration of the Japanned tin was usually the work of women or girls, many of whom may have been related to employees of the firm. As the illustration below indicates, these painters were gifted with good design sense.

Brittania ware became popular during the mid-nineteenth century. Similar to pewter, it was made of tin and antimony with a small amount of zinc, brass and copper. Dover used it almost exclusively for tea and coffee pots.

Of very minor importance then but of great interest today are the Japanned tin toys which Dover offered in its catalogs (and presumably through distributors) throughout the 1800's. It is clear from an examination of the account book of the Union Manufacturing Co. of Clinton, Connecticut, a tin toy manufacturer active in the 1860's, that Dover was not a *complete* producer of tin toys. Union's records list sales to Dover of miniature coffee pots, graters, and tumblers. The models of the toys offered by Dover are also very similar to those of such other Connecticut tin toy manfacturers as Merriam Manufacturing Co. of Durham, Ives of Bridgeport, and Hull and Stafford of Clinton. In some cases, Dover must have been a jobber; in others, it assembled the acquired parts, and/or added their own. It is also possible that they produced miniature, "toy" samples of their standard ware.

What is impressive about Dover is its inventiveness and the durability of its products. With the introduction of a complete line of the French tinned iron, the company provided housewives with truly fine, strong utensils. This is also true of the stove hollow ware. Unfortunately, the company was slow to introduce enameled graniteware which became popular in the 1880's and 1890's. But not until the widespread adoption of aluminum pots and pans in the early 1900's were the company's sales in the utensils market to sag badly.

The firm's inventiveness was very much that of Horace Whitney. The back pages of the 1869 catalog are full of the tinners' tools and machines which he designed and produced. Whitney was also quick to seize upon and offer those other useful inventions patented by others, including C. W. Stow and Roys and Wilcox.

Anyone interested in the Rube Goldberg world of nineteenth-century American tinkering will be delighted by Hershey's "Patent Double Action Apple Parer" pictured on page 112 of the 1869 catalog. It is advertised as "The ONLY MACHINE ever Patented which pares an Apple with the reverse movement of the Knife!" Not as practical as the eggbeater, but the Whitneys who mastered the latter could not resist offering the former. No record exists of how many of Mr. Hershey's product were sold.

It is not unusual, then, that Dover should have been one of the first American stamping companies to install a French double-acting drawing press in their Cambridge plant in 1880. With this press they were able to greatly increase production of tin pans. Introduction of such equipment was a revolutionary event in the American sheet metal industry, and the installation was carried through in the utmost secrecy.

Dover enjoyed halcyon days in the last quarter of the nineteenth century and in the early 1900's. Edward Whitney, son of the founder, succeeded to the presidency of the company in 1883, and several years later the firm was reorganized under the laws of Maine. The company's name was changed to Dover Stamping and Manufacturing Co. The addition "and Manufacturing" was, however, an off-and-on again matter for many years. It was last dropped in the early 1940's.

In 1906 Edward Whitney died and was succeeded by his son, Horace E. who, like his grandfather, was very much of an inventor. Under Horace E. Whitney's direction, the company was drawn more and more into the production of industrial products for the new age of the automobile. Gradually, the firm dropped out of the housewares field. By 1935, two years after the company celebrated its centennial, only a line of pans, plates and eggbeaters was being offered. In the preceding year, Carleton S. Whitney, great-grandson of the founder, had been elected President.

Horace E. Whitney's contribution to the firm was an extensive line of aircraft and automotive supplies—funnels, measures, fillers and oilers—far removed from the colorful world of kitchenware. It was, however, products such as these which kept the company alive during the lean years of the 1930's.

In 1944 it was decided to move the company's base of operations to the empty plant of the General Cotton Supply Company in Fall River, Massachusetts. Whitney Bowen, whose mother was a Whitney, was the owner of the old textile company, and, since the mid-1930's, had been a director of Dover. He became President of the company in 1944, and a year later the move was made.

In 1950 Dover was sold to two industrialists, Sidney Goldstein of Boston and Jacob Ziskand of Fall River. They, in turn, arranged for the sale of the company in 1954 to a company controlled by Louis Berkman, a Steubensville, Ohio, industrialist. Dover is now a division of The Parkersburg Steel Company, one of the companies controlled by Mr. Berkman.

It is a small miracle that the company still exists—and in a prosperous state. It survived countless recessions and several depressions, and almost continuously adapted itself to the furious pace of American economic activity. It must be noted, however, that many of the tinsmiths which Dover supplied managed to stay in business longer than other craftsmen. Henry Kauffman notes in the *Concise Encyclopedia of American Antiques*, that this was "Because he produced a custom-made object involving machine-made parts." If one were to substitute the term "standard-made" for "custom-made," the same principle would hold true for Dover.

For the first fifty years of its existence, Dover was under the direction of one man, and undoubtedly this was a major reason for its strong hold in its field of manufacturing and merchandising. In addition, Horace Whitney and his grandson, Horace E. Whitney, were inventive men, quick to work out and market products which would please housewives who wanted the last word in "scientific" utensils and men who desired the best in hardware and machinery.

Dover continues to produce a catalog, but there is little similarity between it and those of the nineteenth-century. Only two products from the Victorian age survive—wash tubs and coal hods. For the most part, the company is engaged in the manufacture of pails, garbage cans and wastebaskets, items which they market from Northern Maine to Northern Virginia. Dover's past and that of other nineteenth-century tin manufacturers is not, however, being forgotten. Thousands of collectors keep it very much alive.

HORACE WHITNEY

## Suggestions for further reading

COFFIN, MARGARET. *The History and Folklore of American Country Tinware*, 1700–1900. Camden, N.J.: Nelson, 1968.

DeVoe, SHIRLEY SPAULDING. "Japanned Tin-Plate." *The Concise Encyclopedia of American Antiques*, pp. 175–181. New York: Hawthorn, 1965.
*A brief survey of American and English japanning, firms and artisans.*

DeVoe, SHIRLEY SPAULDING. *Tinsmiths of Connecticut.* Middletown, Conn.: Wesleyan, 1968.
*An important and comprehensive history of the most colorful center of tinware manufacturing in America.*

FELT, JOSEPH B. *Customs of New England.* Reprint of the 1853 edition. Detroit, Mich.: Singing Tree.

GOULD, MARY EARLE. *Antique Tin and Tole Ware: Its History and Romance.* Rutland, Vt.: Tuttle, 1958.

GOULD, MARY EARLE. *The Early American House.* Revised edition. Rutland, Vt.: Tuttle, 1965.

JONES, W. H. *Story of Japan and Tin-Plating.* London, 1900.
*Strictly English.*

KAUFFMAN, HENRY J. *Early American Copper, Tin and Brass.* New York: Medill McBride, 1950.

KAUFFMAN, HENRY J. "Tin, Copper and Brass." *The Concise Encyclopedia of American Antiques*, pp. 169–174. New York: Hawthorn, 1965.
*A very brief summary of American tinware.*

Lantz, Louise K. *Old American Kitchenware, 1725–1925.* Camden, N.J.: Nelson, 1970.
*Short sections on tin and Brittania ware. Many illustrations from tinware catalogs.*

Minchinton, W. E. *The British Tinplate Industry, A History.* Oxford: Clarendon Press, 1957.
*A scholarly study which provides interesting information on the nineteenth-century American import market.*

Powers, Beatrice F. and O. Floyd. *Early American Decorated Tinware.* New York: Hastings, 1957.

# Public collections of tinware and other tin objects

The following museums have indicated that they do have within their holdings more than a few pieces of plain tin, Japanned ware, Brittania ware, enameled stove hollow ware, tin toys, or other tin objects of American manufacture in the nineteenth century. Some of these items are on permanent display, others are included in period rooms, and, unfortunately, due to lack of exhibit space, yet others are deep in storage.

No museum—public or private—boasts a substantial collection of *Dover* tinware.

Albany Institute of History and Art, Albany, N.Y.
Chicago Historical Society, Chicago, Ill.
Children's Museum of Indianapolis, Indianapolis, Ind.
Cincinnati Art Museum, Cincinnati, Ohio
Florida State Museum, Gainesville, Fla.
Henry Ford Museum & Greenfield Village, Dearborn, Mich.
Metropolitan Museum, New York, N.Y.
Michigan Historical Commission Museum, Lansing, Mich.
Minnesota Historical Society Museum, St. Paul, Minn.
Missouri Historical Society, St. Louis, Mo.
Museum of History and Industry, Seattle, Wash.
New Jersey Historical Society, Newark, N.J.
New York Historical Society, New York, N.Y.
New York State Historical Association, Cooperstown, N.Y.
Ohio Historical Society, Columbus, Ohio
Old Sturbridge Village, Sturbridge, Mass.
Pennsylvania Farm Museum of Landis Valley, Lancaster, Penn.
Shelburne Museum, Shelburne, Vt.
Smithsonian Institution, Fine Arts Museum, Washington, D.C.
Smithsonian Institution, Museum of History and Technology, Washington, D.C.
South Dakota State Historical Museum, Pierre, S.D.
State Capitol Historical Museum, Olympia, Wash.
State Historical Society of Wisconsin, Madison, Wis.
Staten Island Historical Society, Richmond, S.I., N.Y.
William Penn Memorial Museum, Harrisburg, Penn.
Witte Memorial Museum, San Antonio, Tex.